A Cup of Comfort
for Weddings

Something old,
something new

EDITED BY
HELEN KAY POLASKI

ADAMS MEDIA
Avon, Massachusetts

*This book is dedicated to the couples who understand what it means
to comfort, honor, and keep one another in sickness and in health, for
richer, for poorer, for better, for worse, in sadness and in joy; to cherish
and love, forsaking all others for as long as they both shall live.*

Published by
Adams Media, an F+W Publications Company
57 Littlefield Street, Avon, MA 02322 U.S.A.
www.adamsmedia.com and *www.cupofcomfort.com*

ISBN 10: 1-59337-519-0
ISBN 13: 978-1-59337-519-5

Printed in the United States of America.

J I H G F E D C B A

Library of Congress Cataloging-in-Publication Data
available from the publisher.

*This book is available at quantity discounts for bulk purchases.
For information, please call 1-800-289-0963.*

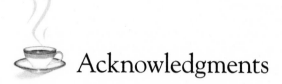 # Acknowledgments

A sincere thank you is extended to my readers, my authors and their families, and to Adams Media. I would also like to thank the Lord for making everything possible.

Contents

 Introduction

I had always imagined I would be married in an apple orchard: soft pink and white blossoms falling down gently, fluffy clouds sailing by in an azure sky as my intended and I gazed into one another's eyes and vowed to cherish and honor until death do us part. It didn't happen quite like that, but I'm not complaining.

The year I turned sixteen, my girlfriend and I went to a neighboring school to watch a basketball game. At one point, the crowd stood up as a young man dropped the ball into the hoop. I stood, too, but my eyes were on a different young man. When the crowd returned to their seats, I remained standing, unable to take my eyes off the boy lounging on the bench, waiting to take his turn in the game.

The people seated nearest me chuckled when I grabbed my best friend's arm and breathlessly said, "See that boy over there—I'm going to marry him."

That starry-eyed magic is what it's all about.

If, like me, you believe in love at first sight and understand that it takes a little bit of magic to keep a couple together 'til death do they part, then this book is for you.

Helen Kay Polaski

The Best of All

The little white church stood proudly with its steeple reaching to the sky, a daily reminder for the farmers in Scarboro, Illinois, that they were not alone.

The little white church was the center of community life. On Sunday, the farmers worshipped there. Monday through Saturday they worked hard. Come spring, they planted. Come summer, *Farmers' Almanac* in hand, they prayed for sunshine, fearing deadly droughts or severe storms with strong winds, both of which challenged their faith that autumn's harvest would be plentiful.

The Lee County house of God stood on a short street along with the grain elevator, a dozen houses, and an old schoolhouse. The church was surrounded by cornfields and bordered by Highways 30 and 51. Fifty-two Sundays a year—barring blizzards—the farmers and their families filled the old oak pews. They bowed their heads in the sanctuary until the final "amen" redirected them to the basement for a smorgasbord of homemade delicacies. Folks of all ages loved the summer picnics and ice cream socials, but weddings were the highlight of the year.

On wedding days the squeaky-clean Chevys and Fords parked every which way on the grass outside. Fathers, their deeply suntanned cheeks contrasting with their bone-white foreheads, climbed out from behind the steering wheels. Smiling mothers whispered final orders to their clan and emerged in flowery dresses with hats to match. Out jumped the farmers' children—more interested in action than appearance. One by one they passed through the open church doors and ascended the steep stairs. Mothers gripped youngsters' hands as they passed the tempting bell rope that dangled above the railing. They filed in, filled the pews, and then waited.

The bells chimed from high up in the white clapboard belfry that joy-filled day in June 1952.

A hundred heads turned so 100 pairs of eyes could watch the dark oak doors swing open. "Here Comes the Bride" was surely the next number to be played in the humble piano's prenuptial medley.

Trying to look inconspicuous, the preacher's daughter hustled in. The seven-year-old girl stood tall, aided by metal-stilt braces that gave height to her tiny size. But the congregation knew the truth. Under the pink dotted swiss dress were malformed legs. Inside the orthopedic shoes were deformed feet, missing toes. There were no secrets in this small town. Everyone knew that inside the white cotton gloves were eight fingers instead of ten.

"She was born that way," a local guest whispered to an out-of-towner who gawked at the child without meaning to be disrespectful. Yet, as always, Judy Ann's confident countenance, buckteeth and all, begot a sanctuary full of honest, bittersweet smiles. The freckled-faced, nine-year-old boy with aquamarine eyes murmured the truth that no one else dared to utter: "Pity the man who marries her."

Many a bride came and many a bride went through that vintage doorway during the lifetime of this little church in America's heartland. But the bell pealed its loudest and proudest in June 1968, as folks from as far east as New York and as far west as California gathered to witness the wedding of the preacher's daughter.

Standing tall on her artificial legs, she resembled a princess bride in her white dotted swiss gown with its 6-foot-long train. Radiating from behind the European lace veil was her perfect smile. Teardrops of wonder dampened cheeks, and 100 souls clapped their hands as 100 pairs of eyes followed the bride step for step down the starched ivory wedding carpet. With one pearl-sequined glove secure on her preacher-father's strong arm, Judy Ann rested her other hand on her daisy-decked cane. Arm in arm, father and daughter threw invisible kisses to a thankful mother in the front pew.

As the wedding march ended, the 100 pairs of eyes contemplated the handsome groom, now a grown lad whose freckles were no more. His aqua-marine eyes were riveted on his bride, and his heart, with a change of tune, sang a new song: "There are many fine women in this world, but you, my love, are the best of all."

Judith Ann Squier

The Little China Cup

I have a little china cup. The handle is gone, the rim chipped, the gilding worn thin. Its faded gold lettering reads: Think of Me. Two dim pink roses wrap around the cup protectively. Time and use have dimmed the colors, but the words remain. The cup is so small I can hold it in the palm of my hand. When I close my fingers gently about the delicate porcelain, it speaks to me of long ago. It makes me think of other lives and other loves and another time.

It has twice been a gift. Robert Benjamine Bishop—Ben, to those who knew him well—bought the little cup as a birthday gift for Annie Roberta McDonald. His sky-blue eyes sparkled in anticipation of seeing his beloved. He had been away for more than a year, having made his way through the Florida wilderness from Madison to Tampa to learn to be a storekeeper. Now he was home at last.

He carefully tied his horse to the post in front of the house, dusted his broadcloth lapels, and straightened his worn straw hat. He reached behind his saddle, into the worn saddlebags, where, swaddled in soft cotton, wrapped in layers of tissue paper, and tied with a precious satin ribbon—pink to match her cheeks—was his homecoming gift to Annie Roberta. The little china cup bore the inscription: Think of Me.

Clutching the package, he hurried through the clean-swept front yard, through the garden—fragrant and glorious in its raiment of roses of every color—and up the wide front steps crafted of Florida cypress. He crossed the veranda of hand-hewn cypress boards and finally arrived at the front door, majestic in its mantle of poured glass. His trip home through the alligator-infested wilds of the untamed country had not seemed half as long as the journey from his horse to the front door of Annie Roberta's home.

Has she forgotten me? Will it be the same? What if she has someone else? The questions drummed inside his head, as they had for months. Soon he would have answers.

Sweat dribbled down his cheeks and down his back as the door opened.

"Miz McD-d-onald!" he said, mortified to hear his own voice break like that of a lad.

"Ben Bishop!" Annie Roberta's mother responded, a smile on her face. "It's a surprise to see you here today."

Mrs. Zillianne Zaradora Phillips McDonald, descendant of Col. Walter Chiles of Jamestown, Virginia, and wife of John Daniel McDonald, was tall, elegant, imposing, and stern, but very kind. She saw the blush begin at Ben's collar and spread over his perspiring face into his soft blond hair. She watched him take a big breath and noticed his white-knuckled grip on a package tied with a pink ribbon.

She smiled. "Won't you come in, our Ben?"

"Thank you, ma'am," Ben said as he followed Miz McDonald down the wide, cool hall and into the splendid Sunday parlor. He only tripped once, on the soft Persian carpet that had come to West Florida by way of a sailing ship around the Horn of Africa. Ben was not normally so tongue-tied and clumsy. Today was special. It was the day he would see his beloved once again and he was nervous beyond belief.

"I'd surely like to see Berta," he said.

"I'll get her for you, Ben," said Miz McDonald. "She's outside in the vegetable patch. I'll get you something cool to drink, as well. You just have a seat for a minute or two."

Ben couldn't sit down. He tried to slow his breathing and tried to calm himself. *What if she doesn't remember? What if she has forgotten me?*

What if she has someone else? He searched the gardens outside the parlor windows for a glimpse of her.

Finally, he heard light footsteps coming down that hall. He turned, and there she was, glossy black braids and laughing gray eyes, carrying a silver tray and two mint-garnished glasses of tea in her hands. When she smiled at him, his world was complete.

She had known he would come back to her. "Oh, my Ben, you have come home—and on my birthday!"

In Ben's eyes, Berta was perfection. He had imagined this as he had trudged for miles through forests thick with panthers, bears, and snakes. He had thought only of her through the heat, the mosquitoes, and the discomfort. All the way home he had rehearsed what he would say. Now that the moment was real, he could not say a word. Finally, he held out his hand and offered the carefully wrapped package.

Berta offered her wonderful grin. "Oh, Ben! You've brought me a present!" She took the gift from Ben's trembling fingers. She untied the satin ribbon and retied it on one of her long silken braids. Then, very carefully, she unwrapped the gift and held it in the palm of her hand. As she read the inscription, a soft smile came to her lips.

They had loved each other all of their lives as children, as neighbors, as friends. And they would continue to love one another as husband and wife.

On March 28, 1907—not long after this—they were married.

Forever after, the little china cup held a place of honor in the parlor of the home that had been a wedding gift to the couple from her father. Years passed, and Ben and Berta had two little girls, Mildred and Elizabeth. As a special treat, the girls were sometimes allowed to use the cup when they held tea parties with imagined royalty. One day, the rim was chipped, although no one ever knew from which little hand it had slipped.

Each year on Berta's birthday, Ben and Berta shared a sip of elderberry wine from the little cup and Ben would whisper, "Ah, my Berta, always think of me." Berta would light his world with her smile, and nod and promise to always think of him.

Then tragedy struck on her birthday in 1912, and they buried Ben. He hadn't been ill but for a day or two. My mother, Elizabeth, was only two and doesn't remember. Aunt Mildred, at four, was heartbroken. That night, Aunt Mildred said Granny took down the little cup and filled it with elderberry wine—as had been hers and Ben's birthday tradition. Granny smiled through her tears and took a sip in remembrance of her Ben.

When I came along, the cup sat on the mantel in Grandmother's living room. I will never forget the day my little brothers took the cup down. The sudden, sharp crack of breaking china brought our world to a stop. Granny—who almost never cried—cried that day, then wrapped the cup in tissue paper and put it away.

When I turned twenty-one, Granny handed me a little package tied with a pink satin bow, the color of her own cheeks, so soft and pink. I untied the bow and retied the ribbon around one of my long braids and opened the tissue paper. Inside, I rediscovered the little china cup. That's when Granny told me the story of her beloved Ben. And we two—my beloved grandmother and I—filled the little cup with secret elderberry wine and shared a sip. It was the last birthday I was to share with her, but not the last time I would sip elderberry wine from a special little china cup and think of my grandmother and the love she had shared with her Ben so many years ago.

Beth Gay

A Worthy Catch

I never imagined I'd fall in love with a fisherman, let alone one who lived in Dundas—a Minnesota town the size of a postage stamp—but when Tom and I met at a party given by mutual friends, the attraction popped instantly. Unfortunately, the distance between our worlds stretched out like the banks of the Mississippi after the spring thaw.

Born and raised in Minneapolis, my metropolitan soul felt lost in the open farmland and small-town way of life. Bred in the heart of the valley, Tom balked at the noise and congestion of the twin cities. But love conquers all boundaries, so eventually Tom reeled me in with a proposal of marriage and lifelong bliss.

Our engagement passed by in a whirlwind as we shared our joy with family and friends, adjusted to the new status of our relationship, and planned for the big day. Tom's mother asked me to participate in a Dundas tradition. On the day before the wedding the Dundas women gathered together and, of all things, went fishing. I balked at the vision of hooks and slimy creatures of the sea but eventually caved in to my mother-in-law-to-be. Leave it to the women in the "Land of 10,000 Lakes" to come up with such an offbeat ritual.

On the day before my wedding, I pried myself out of bed at 5:00 A.M. to drive to Roberds Lake. With bleary eyes and a map in hand, I wound my way through the countryside.

As I approached Roberds Lake, the cool scent rolling off the water drifted in through the car window, sweeping the last trace of sleep from my eyes. I felt energized and ready to take on the world—or at least the fish, even if I didn't have a clue how to catch them.

Two seconds later, however, I wasn't quite sure if I was ready to take on the Dundas women. The parking lot across the street from the resort docks was overflowing. Parked vehicles spilled onto the rural highway for at least 100 feet in either direction. I parked behind the last car and glanced toward the docks where a crowd of flannels and windbreakers huddled en masse.

I edged up to the tail end of the group and searched for a familiar face. Would all these people be at our wedding reception, too? If so, we hadn't planned for nearly enough food. Finally, I caught sight of Tom's mother sitting on the far pier. When I tapped her on the shoulder, she looked up from her fishing pole and a huge grin splashed across her weathered face, lighting it up brighter than the rising sun.

"Allie! You found us." She stood up and handed her rod to a lady seated nearby. "Look everyone, Allie is here!"

A cheer rose up from the women, the simultaneous boom certain to scare away any trace of fish from the area. Someone slipped a flannel blanket over my shoulders and suddenly a swarm of women moved toward me, each one patting a different spot on the blanket. Suddenly, a sharp object pinched my arm. "Ouch!" The exclamation escaped my lips as I whirled around to see the source of the pain and something stung my cheek.

Lures? The women were hanging fishing lures on me! Tears welled up in my eyes and spilled over. "Please stop!" I cried.

At Tom's mother's command to stop, the crowd grew silent. She looked at my cheek and said to a woman in the crowd, "Virginia, run and fetch the first aid kit in my toolbox."

A gouge? On my cheek. The day before my wedding. I felt like I was in *The Twilight Zone*. What type of sadists were these people? Was I supposed to be the wedding bait? What did they plan for an encore—throwing me into the lake?

"Oh Allie, I'm so sorry." Tom's mother looked like the wind had been knocked out of her. "We should have prepared you for this. I'm afraid we got a little carried away."

Still not sure what had just happened, I offered a small shrug. "It's okay," I said. But in my head it was not okay. Who in the heck hung fishing lures on a bride-to-be?

"Perhaps I should explain," she offered as she dabbed at my cheek. "Allie, we're terribly sorry we startled you. I should have explained everything ahead of time. You see the quilt on your shoulders? We patterned and stitched it over the past few months from scraps of Tom's old fishing jackets and childhood clothing."

I glanced down at the blanket. Where I'd seen only flannel before, the intricate pattern and handcrafted designs—stunning with their elaborate beauty—now leapt out at me. An ornate replica of Tom's parents' farm filled one square and an intimate rendition of what appeared to be Tom and me cutting our wedding cake filled another. The blanket was covered in square after square of memories and future blessings. Another gush of tears rolled from my eyes, but they did not stem from the pain of the wound.

"And the lures?"

"They are for luck and prosperity. It's customary to wish your life together to be as abundant with love as the countless number of fish that swim in our lakes, and to provide you with a symbol of the tools that will guide you to catch your fill. Each lure is handmade. They are a reassurance for you that we are here to help. We are your tools."

The sting from the alcohol swab on my cheek paled in comparison to the overwhelming thankfulness welling up in my soul. These women, who hardly knew me, had openly welcomed me into their fold.

What an incredible community I'd stumbled into. Crazy Norwegian fisherwomen or not, they were chock-full of hospitality and heart. I threw my arms around Tom's mother and gave her a big squeeze, hoping to convey my gratitude, not just to her, but to all the women on the pier.

Many years later, Tom and I still live in Dundas. Our beautiful quilt—complete with lures—hangs in a prominent spot on our living room wall as a continued reminder of our family heritage and the town that captured my heart. These days, whenever an engagement is announced, I look forward to helping the women of Dundas assure another new bride that she's a worthy catch.

Barb Webb

Dancing with My Best Friend

My husband and I were alone in our home in Deer Park, Texas. It seemed only a few years ago that the house had bustled with energetic teenagers—the three of them grown now, gone to make their mark on this world. I don't recall the program, but music emanated from the television in the den: a soft melody, slow and foolishly nostalgic.

Eleven months had passed since my hit-and-run accident, and another few weeks since I'd stubbornly relegated the wheelchair and walker to our bedroom. I still required the aid of a cane and waddled like a duck, or, as my physical therapist would laugh and say, a Weeble-Wobble.

I'd spent the afternoon puttering around the house, dusting shelves of family photographs and books, my collection of decorative boxes and knick-knacks—things I could finally reach again without asking for anyone's help. Like so many of the household chores I'd taken for granted before my accident, dusting had become a satisfying task. I was grateful to be alive.

I'm not sure when Wayne entered the room, or how long he'd watched me. He was supposed to be getting ready for work. I do recall the warmth of his hands when they reached for mine, his blunt-tipped fingers long and rough, palms calloused: a working man's hands.

I leaned back and looked into his beautiful eyes, a faded celestial blue I'd always found enchanting, which had been passed on to our grandson, Jacob.

"What are you doing?" I asked.

He pulled me close, slipped his arms around my waist so his hands rested on my hips and whispered into my hair, "I'm dancing with my best friend."

For a woman fond of words, I was speechless. We had met at a dance at the Brazoria County Fairgrounds in October 1966, and we married five months later. I smiled into Wayne's shirt as tears filled my eyes and I tried to swallow the mammoth lump forming in my throat. Silly, I know.

We were married for thirty-eight years now, so it wasn't as though we hadn't danced many times like this, holding tight to one another, swaying to an easygoing rhythm. Nor was this the first time he had called me his best friend. Usually he did it as a reference point in conversations: "My best friend once told me . . . " or "I asked my best friend about that just the other day and she said . . . "

I always knew he meant me. He made sure I knew, with a look or a wink, that disarming smile. But spontaneity had never been Wayne's strong suit. And this dance, this sweet and tender moment was his way of reassuring me, of letting me know that, in spite of the broken bones, banged-up knees, scarred forehead, and the limp that would most likely be permanent, I was going to be okay.

We were okay, and, for that fleeting moment, nothing else mattered. Just us . . . and our dance.

For a man who never embraced romance (except in his favorite movies), a man who bah-humbugged his way through Christmas, who often forgot birthdays and anniversaries and valentines, this brief twirl on an imaginary dance floor was the single most romantic gift he could ever give me. It was better than a dozen daisies, a balloon-filled luxury liner or a trillion Snickers bars.

I needed reassurance, and he knew it. He always knew.

The music ended and we stood there, souls and hearts linked, as they had been almost from the moment we met at that hokey county fair so many years ago. His big hands trembled as they moved from my hips to the middle of my back.

"I've never been so scared as I was that night," he said. "I thought I'd lost you."

I answered simply, "I know, sweetie, I know." But I didn't know. I couldn't begin to fathom the pain he'd suffered or the horror he must've felt the night of the accident—realizing, as we walked through the parking lot, that the speeding car was going to hit me and that he was powerless to prevent it. He'd told me how he hated that he wasn't standing next to me that night, protecting me, instead of walking a few yards ahead as he habitually did.

I thanked God he wasn't standing close to me. I never want to imagine that kind of hopelessness, that infinite helplessness, or ever experience it again. I'd heard enough from our children. At the hospital, they had seen their dad, this rock of a man, cry for the first time in their lives. And his tears shook them.

What I do know—what I've never been more sure of—is that there's more romance in my handsome husband than he would ever admit, and I'm the luckiest woman in the world.

Let other women have their bouquets and trinkets, their exotic cruises and cards and valentines. I'll have my dance.

Sharon Cupp Pennington

Miracle or Coincidence?

It was a turning point in Roger Coletti's life—a miracle, actually. And though it's been more than sixty years since it happened, every detail is still fresh in his mind. The year was 1940 and Roger was in the army. Back home in Beverly, Massachusetts, his sweetheart, Eleanor Kelaher, was training to be a nurse.

Separation was difficult. The couple wrote daily letters, and both looked forward to Roger's upcoming leave. When the day finally arrived, Roger took a train to Boston's South Station and splurged on a taxi to Children's Hospital, where Eleanor was training.

"We didn't have any money back then," he explains. "We went to the nearby Mission Church for the Novena Mass." The church's shrine, Our Lady of Perpetual Help, drew the sick and ailing from the Greater Boston area. They wrote their petitions and lit candles.

"I can remember the beautiful stained-glass windows," says Roger, his face softening with the memory. "Late afternoon—when the sun set—they bathed you in a rosy glow."

When his brief leave ended, Roger returned to his army life. In the months that followed, he moved around quite a bit and his letters to Eleanor became less frequent. Not only that, but he began thinking he was too young for a romantic commitment. After all, they were barely twenty. In that frame of mind, Roger wrote Eleanor and explained as best he could.

"I never felt right about it," he now admits.

Time passed and then one day he received a letter from Eleanor informing him that she had become engaged. Roger sighs. "I knew immediately I'd done the wrong thing."

In the following days, Roger became determined to go home and straighten things out with Eleanor. "It's true that you don't appreciate something until you lose it," he says.

He was so distraught that his weight dropped from 175 to 139 pounds. He counted the days and hours until his discharge. Finally, he boarded a train in El Paso for the five-day trip home.

Roger looks off into the distance as he recalls the trip and the tension he felt. "The ice ponds, as the train sped by, were like a string of pearls."

It had been hot and airless in Texas; his first taste of New England air was invigorating. As the train pulled into South Station, Roger knew where he wanted to go. The Irish cab driver, noting Roger's uniform, said "no charge" when he dropped him at the Mission Church. Roger stepped inside the church, and, taking a deep breath, made his petition. He was heartened by the assortment of crutches left behind at the altar. Perhaps his wishes would be answered.

He went back to the train station and boarded another train for the 20-mile trip that would take him home. When he alighted at Beverly Depot, there was one lone person inside the cavernous station waiting for the train that would go to Boston. Roger still cannot describe how he felt when he realized it was Eleanor sitting there alone on that cold winter afternoon.

When Eleanor's train arrived, Roger boarded it with her. They talked all the way back, and continued when they reached the city. Later, on the return trip to Beverly, they held hands. Needless to say, Eleanor's engagement was no longer paramount in her mind.

Finding Eleanor at the station was Roger's miracle. Following their wedding, he told the story often, especially to their six children. Over time, they got tired of hearing the tale. He, however, never got tired of telling it.

Sharon Love Cook

The Yellow Swimsuit

It was a small, factual article, tucked in among ads for cabbages and carrots and announcements of birthdays and funerals. The headline read: "Fire Partially Destroys Redding's Mill Inn." It had taken two fire trucks to put out the fire. There were no injuries. The upper part of the building was completely destroyed—all went up in smoke.

That was it. There was no mention of the princess or the prince, no mention of the *magic*. But I knew. That old building had been my palace, and I, its Cinderella—complete with a glass slipper . . . of sorts.

In June of 1948, the Inn was called Wimpy's and it was known for its fabulous hamburgers: great monstrous sandwiches, with pickles and thinly sliced onions, wrapped in tissue paper and served in a basket. Cold drinks were served in real glasses.

Wimpy's had a vast, magical dance floor. They sprinkled fairy dust or something on it that made you slip and slide. So with every dance not only was there a chance you would be swept off your feet, it was highly likely. In the middle of the room, a big mirrored ball hung from the ceiling. A light directed up from the floor turned the room into a thing of mysterious beauty. That light made everything sparkle and seem alive. We were in a glass snowball all shaken up. We chased those swirling snowflakes of lights as we glided across that floor. And some-times—between the swirls of light—we stole a kiss and our dreams came true.

Saturday afternoons were spent at Wimpy's. We'd drink Cokes, eat hamburgers and french-fries, play pinball, and disappear onto the dance floor. Later in the afternoon, we would head for Sagamount, just down the road. It was an oasis that boasted three swimming pools.

That summer, the boys—our knights in shining armor—started coming back from World War II. Life began to take on new flavors that had been rationed during the war. There was one particular flavor that was extra special. His name was Jack, and I was very interested in him. And needing to know everything about him, I turned into my own spy. Each bit of information was handled like valuable intelligence. I couldn't get enough. I was gathering twigs and sticks for a nest. As we began to learn what made each other tick, I found that, among other things, his favorite color was yellow.

That was all I needed to know. The next afternoon, my sister and I went on a mission to Ramsay's Department store. We shopped for a new bathing suit for me. I explained to the clerk that only one color would do. I needed a yellow bathing suit, and no one questions a royal request from the princess.

That Saturday it was the usual. We went to Wimpy's for lunch along with my sister and her boyfriend. We put our quarters in the jukebox. At that time, you got a bargain: six plays for a quarter. We danced to our favorite tunes, "Stardust" and "String of Pearls." Then we jumped into Jack's Nash Rambler and made way to our destination: Sagamount. I could hardly wait to put on my new yellow swimsuit.

The sun was fierce that day. After a while, thinking about how perfectly things were going, I jumped into the pool to cool off. As soon as I climbed up the ladder and out of the water, my sister turned into a maniac. She jumped up and down and yelled to get my attention. I smiled and waved back, thinking about how good I must look in my yellow suit. I glanced around looking for Jack. I saw him lounging against the side of the pool with a silly little grin playing about his mouth—but he would not look at me directly.

At that moment, my sister shrieked at the top of her lungs, "To the dressing room! NOW!"

I looked at her and frowned, but I'd heard that tone before. Whatever was going on, she wasn't joking. I stepped around the edge of the pool and made my way into the dimly lit dressing room, where I waited for her. As soon as she entered, she pushed me in front of the full-length mirror. What had been a yellow bathing suit now had *no* color. Like Cinderella's glass slipper, it was invisible—but I certainly was not!

We quickly dressed, grabbed our swimming gear, and headed back to Wimpy's. My sister and my friends tried to soothe my ruffled feathers. They assured me that any self-respecting store would refund the cost of the yellow bathing suit if I told them my sad story.

I just looked at them and swallowed the lump in my throat. They had no clue that this was not what I was worried about. They didn't know I had been gathering twigs and sticks.

As the afternoon progressed, I managed to keep my tears at bay, though I did notice that Jack was a little different. While we danced a little closer than usual, we also talked a lot more than normal. I learned that besides yellow he liked people, dogs, fishing, and beer.

By July 16 we were engaged. We tied the knot that September.

So now as I look at the article that had originally caught my eye, maybe it isn't so factual after all. Maybe there was more to be told of that old building: the dance floor, a princess, her prince, and magic. And maybe it all didn't go up in smoke, because the magic still lingers in my heart. And the moral of the story is that when a princess gathers sticks and twigs and can't find a glass slipper, maybe she just needs to grab a yellow swimsuit and go swimming. In my case, it was a guarantee of much magic to follow.

Dorothy Scearcy

The Flash of a Smile

I met Phillip while I was trying to get rid of Jacob, my latest boyfriend, a full-lipped boy who played the trombone at a neighboring church. At that time, parents connived who their children might encounter as possible mates—long before hormones kicked in—but it was all done rather hush-hush. Jacob's mother had called Mama a week before my seventeenth birthday, and before I knew it, they were in our dining room eating Sunday fried chicken. Set up from the get-go, I sat between Jacob and his red hair and his mama with her black hair spun on her head like cotton candy. The two mamas approved. I had no say-so. They let him take me out.

I came home from our first date determined that our second date would be our last. Mama asked me how it went, her face full of hope.

"Nice, real nice," I said as I fell into bed, clothes and all.

On our second date, Jacob and I met the youth group after church at Marcello's Pizza House and claimed a booth. Only a few minutes had passed when the door opened and a tall, dusty-blond guy wearing worn jeans walked in. He moved in our direction and slid into the booth across from us. He said hi to Jacob and nodded at me. Jacob introduced him as his best friend, Phillip. Phillip smiled at me with intense blue eyes and a flash of a smile. I smiled back, swallowed hard, and scooted away from Jacob.

Phillip smoothed out his mustache by separating his thumb and forefinger across his lip. I'd never been kissed by a boy with a mustache.

"Did yous eats?" He talked funny. Maybe he's foreign, I thought. I lifted one arm onto the table and leaned one shoulder slightly in to let my elbow-length brown hair play across my arm. I made sure to keep up the chitchat long enough to make an impression—laying it on as thick as cream-cheese icing on red velvet cake. I decided that Phillip was too muscular and his face too old for him to still be in high school. I couldn't wait to get home and call my best friend to tell her about this new guy with a mustache and a foreign accent.

Phillip turned out to be from Cincinnati, Ohio, not France as I had imagined. I also found out he was twenty-two. I was barely seventeen. Mama wasn't going to like that, but at least he attended the same church.

Phillip and I spent the next year falling deeper and deeper in love, and we planned to get married after I turned eighteen.

On the day of my wedding, Daddy stood in the vestibule of Northeast Assembly of God, decked out in his blue suit, looking hot and uncomfortable. I walked up in my wedding dress and veil. He smiled and then his lips began to quiver. I picked up a red rose and pinned it on his lapel. His mouth constantly moved in an attempt to hold back the tears. I grabbed the crook of his arm and he gave a squeeze just like when I was a little girl nestled beside him in church.

As we stood there, arm in arm, we heard the singer finish the Lord's Prayer and the usher began to open the double doors. Suddenly, Daddy put his hand on the door and turned to me.

"If you're not sure he's the one, I mean, if you don't love him . . . If you have any doubts—any doubts whatsoever—I can take you out of this here church and you'll never have to see him again." He searched my face for the truth.

I looked him square in the eyes. "Yes, Daddy, I love him. He's the one."

"If he ever hurts you . . . if he ever lays one hand on you . . . "

"I know, Daddy. I've always loved you . . . "

The doors opened, heads turned, and I took in a deep breath. Phillip stood at the end of the aisle in a blue suit that matched Daddy's and a huge grin on his face that made me laugh. Without hesitation, I took my first step toward him on my Daddy's arm.

The rest of the day was a frenzy of pictures, cake, presents, and hugs and handshakes. While everyone laughed and ate cake, I realized that I had left my bouquet upstairs. Wanting a moment away from the crowd, I slipped up the back stairs.

Daddy sat in the front pew of the empty church. He sat staring at the altar where Phillip and I had knelt and said our vows. I watched my daddy's massive body curve over onto his knees, his shoulders heaving as he wept.

I stood at the door and looked at Daddy, then thought of Phillip, waiting downstairs for me, and felt blessed to be so loved.

Carol O'Dell

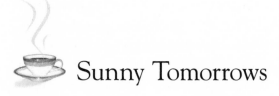

Sunny Tomorrows

When Catherine and I told my Aunt Viola and Uncle Les that we were to be married in September 1953, they immediately offered us their house while they wintered in Clearwater, Florida. I had spent four years in the navy and would be starting college at Boston University a week after our marriage; money would be tight. The offer of their house for $50 a month—the cost of utilities—was too good to be true. But Uncle Les said it would be reassuring to know that we would be taking good care of their house while they were sunning in Florida. Then he winked and said we would be surprised by how little snow we would get this close to the water. His generous offer ended with a big smile.

When we moved in, we felt like Hansel and Gretel. The walk was not strewn with gumdrops, but it might as well have been. From the front, the two-bedroom cottage at 76 Triton Street on Point Shirley in Winthrop, Massachusetts, seemed so small you could almost reach the roof by standing on tiptoes. The tiny cottage overlooked the bay and was perfect both inside and out.

We took the far bedroom as our own. The window overlooking the bay made up our minds for us. The view was beautiful. It was made more perfect by the fact that it belonged to us alone.

Our routine that winter was hectic, and we enjoyed every minute we had to ourselves. Catherine was a surgical nurse and had to be at the bus stop no later than 6:00 A.M. to arrive at the hospital on time. It wasn't long before the morning bus driver recognized her white nurse's stockings and her schedule. He was a good sort, and never hesitated to wait a minute or two if she was running late. My job was to get to class.

One cold winter morning we awoke to discover that the front doorway was filled to the top with snow. It was a big surprise, and we couldn't help wondering whether this was the joke that had led to Uncle Les's parting smile.

When the snow finally melted, the rains came. And along with the rains came the need to spread our wings and invite our first guests over for dinner. Joe Driscoll was a boyhood friend who also had been in the navy. He and his fiancée, Norma, were to be married the following June. The rain beat down all day, but we were too busy having a wonderful time with our friends to give it much thought, until that evening. The cottage was located on a hill, and there was only one road leading back to town. When I finally decided to make a few phone calls, I discovered the road was impassable. Joe and Norma would have to spend the night.

True to form, Catherine refused to let a little rain get us down. The next morning, she insisted on walking down to Pulsiver's Market to pick up eggs and bacon for our breakfast. To her surprise, the street leading to the market was knee-deep in water. A couple of enterprising youngsters with a small boat were offering ten cents a ride to the store, but Catherine, always the adventurous sort, declined and waded through the icy water instead.

As my darling wife drudged back up the hill a half hour later, sopping wet, she saw me in the window and waved cheerfully. It was as if her smile had coaxed the sun from its hiding place, for it rose behind her like a harbinger of good things to come. And that is how I have always remembered 76 Triton Street: a magical place that promised our tomorrows would always be bright.

Ed Boyd

The Letter

When our son David met Lisa at Heidelburg College in Tiffin, Ohio, we had a feeling this young lady might be the light of his life. We were right. The mention of wedding plans surfaced long before they had put their college years behind them. The date was set for late May, shortly after Lisa graduated.

When the time came, everything was perfect that Saturday morning. St. Bernard Catholic Church was majestic; its spires reached for the sky, reminding me of the church of my youth. Sunlight poured in through the stained-glass windows, casting a warm glow to the interior. It was as if the sun was peeking in the windows, hoping for a glimpse of the happy new couple.

The ceremony was beautiful, but it was over much too quickly for my tastes. I watched with a catch in my throat and tears in my eyes as the bridal party clambered up onto a hay wagon and was transported to the hall. My son and his new bride drove away slowly, like a king and queen atop hay bales.

When I arrived at the hall, I spied a beautiful flower arrangement on the gift table and immediately stuck my nose into the red roses, breathing deeply. I was surprised to read that the card was addressed to me. When I saw my son's name, I smiled and tucked the card into my purse to read later.

As the reception ended, the next chapter in my son's life had begun. And with this realization came another catch in my throat. Keeping the tears at bay, I walked to the gift table and picked up my gorgeous vase of roses. As soon as my husband and I arrived at the hotel, I pulled out the card lovingly penned by my son.

It is hard to find words that give justice to the feelings I have today. You have given me more than I will ever be able to repay. You have given me joy. You have given me laughter. You have given me sorrow. You have always been my greatest ally (at times my worst enemy). You have been my friend. You have been my teacher. You have taught me how to live, how to teach others, how to make an impact, and how to make a difference. You have taught me how to love, have given me all that you are, and have carried me when I couldn't walk. You have given me hope, faith, and you have shared your soul with me. You have always made things better no matter how bad things got. You always listened and understood. You have always been by my side (not too close when I needed room). You have been my strength to step out. You have always been my courage and pushed me when I needed it. You have been my smile when I could not. You have cried for me when I could not. You have given me the best twenty-three years of my life, through thick and thin. You have been the one who I could always count on. You have been and will always be my Mom.

The hardest part of love is letting go. Love will be the tie that binds us to the times we leave behind us and these memories will be our souvenirs.

So pray for me, Mom, and I will pray for you. It is time for me to be the person you have been helping to create. The final page has been written and this book is closing but, don't worry! You will be playing a big role in the sequel (just a different role). Don't worry. Lisa is going to take good care of me. The best thing you have taught me is how to love and be loved. Thanks for everything Mom. Hugs and kisses from your son.

I will love you forever,

Dave

The tears I had kept in check all night now flowed from me like a river. I looked at the beautiful roses through tear-filled eyes and smiled my appreciation. Knowing that my son had taken the time to think about me on his special day was a wonderful and unexpected gift, but knowing we had raised a boy who had grown into such a wonderful man was the best gift of all.

Kristine Ziemnik

Saving Pennies

Virginia and Frankie were both born during the 1920s in Newburgh, New York. They were very much alike but lived on opposite ends of the city and were not aware of each other until their teens.

Although spare change was hard to come by in the 1930s, both Virginia and Frankie would save pennies to purchase candy for the orphans who lived in a home for unwanted children just above the Hudson River.

One day as Virginia left the girls' home, she saw a young boy sitting on the sidewalk. With a heavy heart, she explained that she didn't have any candy left to give him. The young boy smiled.

"It's okay," he explained. "Frankie brings us candy. He's the boy over there in the field by the YMCA."

Curious, Virginia walked with the young boy toward the fence and peeked through. On the other side, she spotted a slender youth with a pole in his hands. He spotted her, too, and with the vaulting pole extended, leapt over the fence, landing in front of her.

"Hi there," he said cheerfully. "I'm Frank. Who are you?"

Virginia's father was a tough old guy and refused to allow his sixteen-year-old daughter to go out on a date, especially when she was talking about a boy from the other side of town. It took many months and much persuasion, but he finally relented and Virginia was allowed to go to the movies with her new beau. Of course, they would need a chaperone, a job Virginia's mother happily accepted. In those days, the ten-cent admission included a movie and a dinner plate. Today, the plates are better known as Depression glass and are worth a fortune—but back then they were used as everyday dishes, and Virginia's mother was happy with her growing collection.

After several years and many movies, Frankie finally got up the nerve and asked Virginia's dad for her hand in marriage. In the 1940s there seldom were large wedding celebrations of the type we enjoy today, yet Virginia and Frankie celebrated their union with the grandest of celebrations. No one could afford to bring a gift to the reception, save for one teakettle that was given by an aunt. The dancing was limited to the one fast song on the jukebox, "I've Got Bells That Jingle, Jangle, Jingle," yet no one seemed to mind—especially not the bride and groom.

Over the years, they marveled how an introduction on behalf of a small child had led to a romance
that spanned sixty-seven years, cultivating sixty-two
years of marriage, four children, six grandchildren,
and seven great-grandchildren. Surely, they thought,
things happen for a reason.

With that in mind, it had to be fate that inter-
vened on that Sunday afternoon in July 2004 when
my husband and I took my parents to dinner to
celebrate their anniversary. As we entered the restaurant, a seventy-five-year-old gentleman approached
my father.

"Hi, Frankie," he said in greeting. "How've you
been?"

Tears filled my father's eyes, and I turned to my
mother in puzzlement. She smiled, dabbing at her
eyes, and said quietly, "That gentleman was the same
orphan boy who introduced me to your father so
many years ago."

The gentleman gripped my father's hand tightly.
"You remember me, don't you, Frankie?"

I watched in surprise as my father, too, dabbed at
his eyes, then turned around and found my mother's
hand and pulled her forward gently.

"Virginia, look who's here . . . "

Michele Starkey

 Finicky Bride

In 1984, I graduated from high school, enrolled at a local community college, and accepted an engagement ring at Christmas from my boyfriend of one year.

Getting married at a young age was simply what girls did in my small community in northeast Alabama. My mother had married at the naive age of sixteen back in 1946, and both my older sisters had tied the knot while still in their teens.

I had always dreamed of being a June bride, so plans were quickly set into motion for an elaborate wedding. There were no local bridal shops, so on a cold Saturday in January, my mother, two sisters, and I traveled to Huntsville, a larger city nearby. I had a good feeling that the dress of my dreams would accompany us home in the backseat of my car that day. However, by late afternoon there was still no sign of the gown that would play the leading role on my special occasion. My sisters suggested we call it a day and try again the following week.

I was despondent as we drove out of town, but when we passed a small building with snowy white gowns in the window, I coerced everyone into stopping.

Inside, the old-fashioned establishment smelled like a bouquet of fresh-cut flowers. The petite owner was ecstatic to showcase her wares as she trailed behind us, pointing out various gowns. While there were many gorgeous selections in my size, none caught my eye. Mom quietly whispered to my sisters that I was "being finicky," but I ignored them and dejectedly walked toward the exit.

The shop owner called out that she had some new arrivals in the back and there was one that she thought I might be interested in. Leaving no stone unturned, I agreed to take a look. When she returned with the vision in white, I couldn't squelch my enthusiasm. It was the dress I had been searching for all day!

Without checking the size, I raced to the fitting room to try it on. Even though it was too large, I was confident it was the dress for me. The shop didn't offer alterations, but I was positive it could be resized in my hometown.

I hit rock bottom the following Monday morning when a local sewing shop told me there was no way the wedding gown could be altered because of the hundreds of hand-sewn pearls and sequins covering the bodice. The following day, a friend told me about a woman she once knew who had a sewing machine set up in a small room at the back of her house. The home alterations shop wasn't advertised in the telephone directory, but after a few calls to some acquaintances, I finally located the number.

My mother and I drove across town that same day and easily located the modest white house on a large, shady lot. A friendly smile greeted us at the screen door, and Peggy quickly made us feel at home. I removed the dress from the garment bag and she carefully inspected it before asking me to step into the next room and try it on. When I emerged, she put a handful of straight pins into the shoulders and sides of my dress and told me that it would be ready to pick up in two days.

I breathed a deep sigh of relief when I returned at the allotted time and my dress was unveiled. It looked just as beautiful, only smaller. I quickly tried it on and tears of joy filled my eyes. The gown looked as if it had been custom-made for me. I eagerly thanked the sewing lady and paid her the few dollars she insisted was all I owed her.

A few weeks later, on Valentine's Day, my fiancé didn't arrive on my doorstep with roses and chocolates. He telephoned instead and announced none too gently that he wasn't ready to get married.

"You'll take care of canceling all of the wedding plans, won't you?" he asked with a hasty apology.

I cried, I raged, and then I cried some more. I was heartbroken, but my family tried to tell me that it was probably for the best. Days passed into weeks and weeks merged into months. Although I was doubtful at times, life went on and I survived.

While at the supermarket in the fall of that same year, I ran into Peggy, the lady who had altered my dress a few months prior. She wanted all of the details of my wedding and especially wanted to see a photograph of me in my gown. She was sympathetic when I told her that my fiancé had called the whole thing off.

Before leaving, I thanked her once again for the beautiful job she had done on my wedding gown. I assured her that it was carefully bagged and stored and awaiting the day I would wear it while walking down the aisle on the arm of my real "Mister Right." With a sparkle in her eye, she began telling me about her son, Tim. He wasn't married and, according to her, was the best catch in town. I wasn't interested in dating anyone again, especially a guy who would allow his mother to make dates for him. But Peggy was very convincing and somehow managed to talk me into meeting him.

A year later, I did have my perfect summer wedding. I wore the dress of my dreams while standing beside Tim, the blind date with whom I have shared the last nineteen years of my life, in the same small town where we met and fell in love.

I shudder to think of where I might have ended up had I not started out as a finicky bride and set the wheels of fate into motion that day so very long ago.

Sandy Williams Driver

Grandpa Doesn't Eat Carrots

The first meal Grandma prepared her new husband was a pot roast with a thick brown gravy, mashed potatoes, green beans, and candied carrots. He was not unkind with his words, but he pushed the latter to the side of the plate and gently said, "I don't eat carrots."

"It must have been the way I prepared them," Grandma thought. She loved carrots. Surely she wasn't supposed to give them up. She added carrots, potatoes, and onions into the next pot roast she prepared, but Grandpa pushed the carrots to the side of his plate. "I don't eat carrots," he explained a second time.

There was little else they disagreed on, and the things that fell into that category were quickly discussed, compromises made, and life went on. But Grandma loved carrots and continuously looked for a way to serve them that wouldn't offend her husband.

When she shaved carrots over a salad, it drew the same comment: "I don't eat carrots."

Grandma and Grandpa grew a huge garden, and a pair of cottontails and a roadrunner took to watching them from a very close vantage point. The animals didn't bother the garden; they didn't have to because Grandpa left tidbits for them over to the side. The tidbits never included carrots, of course, for carrots were never planted in Grandpa's garden.

One day, Grandma had a craving for carrots. Wondering how she could make her favorite vegetable without offending her husband, she had an idea. She made carrot cake. When Grandpa asked what kind of cake it was, Grandma smiled and told him it was a spice cake. Grandpa *loved* the cake. There was no quick "I told you so" from Grandma's lips. She was far too much of a lady for that.

Grandma's special spice cake quickly became Grandpa's favorite dessert. In more than fifty years of marriage it never dawned on him that he was far more likely to get his favorite cake immediately after they had a small disagreement than if he had performed a thoughtful act. The significance went unnoticed. And as the years passed, Grandma never saw reason to tell Grandpa that her specialty cake was actually carrot cake. She was above that. Besides, Grandpa never bothered to ask. He, in his role as the head of the house, was content in the knowledge that his wife made the best darn dessert in the county.

Grandma smiled serenely each time Grandpa pushed yet another serving of carrots to the side of his plate. She knew in a moment he would launch into her spice cake with relish, and there was much satisfaction in knowing that his treat was not nearly as rewarding as was her quiet victory.

Terry Burns

In Sickness and in Health

They say love heals all wounds, but I had never heard of love curing cancer.

My fingers tightened around the sheet of paper. Two words jumped out at me from the striped page and bore into my brain. More times than not, these two words heralded the kiss of death: Myeloproliferative syndrome. In layman's terms: bone-marrow cancer.

At twenty-nine years of age, I had so much for which to be thankful: a wonderful job as a medical secretary, a loving family, and a new boyfriend who treated me with the utmost respect—I was on top of the world. How dare some dreaded disease infest my lifeblood and rob me?

Normally, I would have avoided my next birthday at all costs. Funny how those two words made me want to experience birthdays well past my thirtieth. Despite the papers in my hands, I vowed to make every day more memorable than the previous day. Depression and despair were banned from my vocabulary.

A few days later, my mother accompanied me to the oncologist's office. Around me sat people with sullen expressions wearing scarves and baseball caps. My vanity surfaced and I touched my hair lightly. Taking a deep breath, I pulled my planner from my leather bag. Seeing my agitation, my mother placed a kiss on my cheek.

"Everything will be fine," she said.

I shoved the planner back into the leather depths of the bag and glanced out the bay window. In that instant, I saw a pickup truck slide into a parking place. A few seconds later, the door at the main entrance opened, and all six feet, eight inches of my smiling real-life hero strode into view. Dave sat down beside me and pulled me close.

"You're going to be okay," he said reassuringly. "No matter what, we're going to get through this." Warmth flooded my body. His breath fanned against my cheek, and his hands enfolded mine. I smiled at my mother and at Dave. We were truly a united front.

Dave's fingers traced over the ring finger of my left hand. "Forever and ever . . . till the end and back again," he said. I looked at him with misty eyes. If anyone could stop this from happening, Dave could.

As if reading my mind, he added, "We're going to be together for a long time. I'm not giving up on you. Nothing's going to happen."

A few minutes later, the nurse called my name. For five years, I'd served in various clinical and clerical positions in a medical office. Today, the walls of a once-familiar setting were closing in around me. Uncertainty clawed at my consciousness, and long before I was ready for real battle, I had entered the oncologist's office and the door closed behind me.

The specialist discussed the potential course of my illness at length, taking time to make sure I understood what he was saying. I glanced at his desk. Various labs and diagnostic tests were spread across his desk blotter. He perused them from time to time. I looked toward the window as sunlight streamed through the vertical blinds.

The kind physician smiled gently at my anxiety. "Did they perform a monospot on you at any time?" he asked. When I said no, he escorted me to the lab.

Two vials of blood were drawn, and then I was asked to return to the waiting room. My mother laced her fingers through the fingers on my right hand, and Dave claimed the left. After a while, Dave leaned over and whispered, "I love you." Something about the way he said it made me realize that he would be the man who'd walk with me down the wedding aisle.

Only a short time had elapsed before the nurse called me back to meet with the oncologist again. The moment I saw his grin, my world ceased tipping on its axis.

"You have mono," he said, his smile widening.

I did not have cancer.

That evening, Dave brought over an armload of games and arranged them on the living room floor. Until my mono cleared, he visited and entertained me without fail. He even watched chick flicks with me and never complained. In short, he put his life on hold for me. But the moment I remember most during those games wasn't a game at all, but reality. I felt our love crackle in the air surrounding us.

One evening in July, as we stood on my porch together watching the dappled midnight sky in wonder, he took my hands, held them to his lips, and kissed them.

His voice was soft as he whispered, "I love you. Today. Tomorrow. Always. I'm here to stay."

More than ten years later, Dave is still a driving force in my life. We'll celebrate our ninth wedding anniversary this spring. One very big positive came out of that very negative-sounding preliminary diagnosis—true love.

Kimberly Shoemaker

The Friendship Quilt

"Tell me about the friendship quilt, Grandmother," I begged.

When I was growing up in Wild Horse Creek, Arkansas, this particular family story was my favorite, for it evoked my grandparents' youth, their courtship, and their marriage.

My grandmother, Katherine Hughs, was only eighteen when she married my grandfather, Thomas Thompson, who was twelve years her senior. They met in Yell County, Arkansas, during those turbulent times that followed the Civil War. Thomas lost four uncles as well as his father in the bloody conflict, and Katherine's father never fully recovered from the physical and emotional wounds he was left with after the war was finally declared over.

Thomas had "cut a wide swath," dating girls all over Logan and Yell Counties. Grandmother's bold and free-spirited older sister, Victoria Hughs, also had pursued Thomas, but when he chose a bride, it was Victoria's shy younger sister, Katherine.

On a bright October Sunday, Katherine and Thomas were married following the church service in Chickalah, Arkansas. Thomas was handsome in his father's black suit, the sleeves only a little too short, and Katherine was radiant in a blue paisley dress that matched her eyes.

The young couple moved into Thomas's mother's cabin while she went to visit her married daughters. But after a year of working the small farm, Thomas set his sights on moving to the Chickasaw Nation, where land was plentiful and cheap. Katherine, now pregnant, remained in Arkansas until he had found a place for them to live.

It was during that lonely separation that the friendship quilt became part of our family lore. Katherine had just washed the breakfast dishes one morning when she heard carriage wheels and the sound of laughter. She opened the door to find two strikingly pretty women standing on her front porch, holding a large package. Grandma said she had never felt more awkward and ugly as their curious eyes appraised her bulky figure.

"Good morning, Katherine Thompson," one of the ladies said sweetly. "We heard you are going out to the Territory soon to join Thomas. It's our custom in Chickalah to give a friendship quilt as a going-away gift." With that, the two women unrolled the quilt. Although it was a beautiful handmade quilt, when Katherine's eyes took in the detail, she had to swallow hard to keep from choking outright.

The quilt was embroidered with forget-me-nots and was made up of sixteen different squares of material. All sixteen squares had been adorned with the names of girls Thomas had dated prior to his marriage. Katherine had not known there were so many. And though she recognized all of the names, it was the last name that burned a hole in her heart: Victoria. Only days after Katherine and Thomas had tied the knot, Victoria eloped with an elderly neighbor and moved west into the Territory. Katherine knew she would never see her sister again, for Victoria was shot and killed near Tecumseh, shortly after Oklahoma became a state.

Always at this point in the narrative, my grandmother grew pensive. To divert her, I would ask, "But what happened to the friendship quilt? It looks like a plain old double wedding ring quilt to me."

Grandmother would smile and say, "Well, I wanted to throw it away, but we had very little bedding and I knew winters would be cold in the Chickasaw Nation. So I packed it in the trunk that traveled with me when I went West to join your grandfather. He had found a piece of land and built us a sod house in what would soon become the new state of Oklahoma."

Grandpa had laughed uproariously when he first saw the friendship quilt. "Can you imagine those gals doing this for us, Katherine?"

Grandma was silent. She knew why the gals had made the hateful quilt. It had nothing to do with her—they had wanted Thomas to remember them. And since she had kept it, she would use it, which caused one of her biggest dilemmas. If she put the quilt right side up on their bed, the names of all of those gals stared at her. If she turned it wrong side out, on cold winter nights the names, especially Victoria's name, burned into her flesh. Over the next year, she patiently worked each night by lamplight, piecing together a double wedding ring quilt top, which she then quilted over the friendship quilt.

Each time she got to this point in the story, I had to smile. For some reason, this was the part that delighted me the most. Perhaps it was because I knew in my heart that my grandmother—who didn't have a mean bone in her body—was able to get the last word. What better way to prove that she had won but to place the symbols of her and Thomas's love over the names of the women who had hoped to win her husband's love?

The first time she told me the story, I stared at her with wide eyes. "Do you mean if I tore away the top, all those names would still be there?" I asked.

"So far as I know, child," she said with a soft smile. "But I plan to keep them hidden away. Those names aren't a bit more agreeable to me now than they were back in 1895!"

By the time I was born, Grandmother's friend-ship quilt had turned faded and worn, but it always lay across the foot of her bed—never far away.

When at last she moved to a tiny room at the Shady Rest Nursing Home, the friendship quilt was one of the few possessions she took with her.

"But, Grandma," I had asked her, somewhat con-fused, "if those names are so offensive to you, why have you carried this quilt all over Oklahoma and brought it here to Shady Rest?"

My grandmother's face was radiant as she answered slowly, "Oh, Kathryn Jane, sweet child, when you are as old as I am, you will understand that some of the hardest things in life become the most precious. This quilt is like that. I wish Thomas hadn't dated all those wild, silly girls—especially my sister, Victoria. But he was faithful to me for all the years that remained to him. And this quilt reminds me of cold nights in the soddy and sitting up with sick children."

Her eyes grew misty as she continued. "We lost little Will in that awful flu epidemic." She looked at me with blue eyes as faded as the quilt. "There's so much joy and sorrow in this quilt that it's become a part of me. I hope one day you will cherish it as much as I do."

A few weeks later, I went to my grandmother's funeral. She left me her Bible and a dainty lace handkerchief, but the old quilt had vanished from the Shady Rest Nursing Home. No one can remember seeing it again after she died. Perhaps it had been tucked in around my grandmother's legs, to remain with her always, or perhaps on winter nights, the friendship quilt is still out there somewhere, warming sleeping children and keeping a marriage strong.

Kathryn Thompson Presley

Blind Date

The year was 1950 and I was a busy man. One day as I sat in my office, focused on a stack of paperwork, the telephone began to ring. It had been eighteen months since the death of my wife Sarah, and I had sought solace and distraction in work. A ringing telephone had become a source of resentment to me, rather than a business asset. If I worked long enough and hard enough, I was able to sleep a few hours at night. Anything, like a ringing telephone, that took my mind off my work angered me. On the sixth ring, I finally answered the phone and unknowingly set into motion an event that would change my life forever.

The caller was my longtime buddy, Sam. Sarah and I, and Sam and his wife, Maggie, had enjoyed many years of fellowship and shared activities. But since Sarah's death, I had distanced myself from Sam and all of his family. Seeing them brought back too many bittersweet and painful memories. In fact, I avoided anything that reminded me of Sarah.

"Hey, old buddy," he said, "I really need a favor. You know I've done a few for you over the years, and I'm calling in a marker. Maggie's sister, a widow, just moved to town. She's very lonely." An irritated sigh hissed from my mouth, and upon hearing it, Sam rushed to finish his speech. "Now, before you say anything, let me tell you this chick, named Mitzi, is beautiful, smart, and interesting. All I want you to do is meet us at her apartment tonight. We'll all visit for a little while, then go to the country club. I hear they booked an outstanding band."

Exasperated, I snapped, "Sam, are you trying to set me up on a blind date with your sister-in-law? I just can't believe you'd pull such an underhanded trick. I'm fifty years old! I was lucky in love once. That could never happen again, certainly not at my age. No one could take Sarah's place in my life— some friend you are." I was so upset it was all I could do to keep a civil tongue in my head. "You make it awkward to say no, but I'm saying no anyway!"

On the end of the receiver, it was Sam's turn to sigh in frustration. "Now wait," he said. "Would I lie to you? She's a great lady and you'll hate yourself later if you miss this opportunity. I'm not suggesting you marry her. Just meet her and get acquainted."

There was a pause, and then Sam added, "Tell you what. When we get to the club—if you can't stand her—we'll make up some excuse for you to leave and I'll harbor no hard feelings. I'll understand."

Later that night, against my better judgment, I rang her doorbell. She opened the door and looked straight at my belt buckle. I stared down on the top of her head. I'm six feet five inches tall and she is only five feet two inches tall, which made things a bit awkward.

After recovering from the initial shock, we exchanged names and greetings, and she invited me in for a glass of wine and a get-acquainted chat while we waited for Sam and Maggie.

I saw immediately that my buddy's description of this little lady was grossly understated. To me, she was perfection. And to my delight it wasn't just her beauty that swept me off my feet. We had so much in common it was as if we were soul mates.

We enjoyed the same types of books and shared favorite authors. We liked the same ethnic foods, cheered for the same sports teams, and were members of the same church denomination. We both had recently lost our spouses and had wallowed in our grief and loneliness, making no effort to adjust.

An emergency at our local hospital, where Sam is a physician, created an hour delay for him, and by the time Sam and Maggie had arrived, Mitzi and I felt like old friends. We agreed to make one concession to the height difference by declining the country club dance, opting for a movie instead. Sam and Maggie voiced no objection.

Sometimes blind dates produce disastrous results, but not this time. Mitzi and I both felt we had been given a second chance. Without hesitation, we grabbed the brass ring and soon replaced it with a set of wedding bands. Twenty-five years later, we are still as happy as we were the day my friend Sam cared enough to arrange a very special blind date.

Jim Wilson, as told to Pat Capps Mehaffey

Blessed Be the Hem That Binds

When I was a girl in the genteel South, my large and loving family lived on the outskirts of Pensacola, Florida, which at the time might as well have been the end of the world. Folks with any sense, in town and out, knew better than to invite a family of nine children anywhere. An invitation to a wedding seemed unimaginably grand.

So I felt doubly blessed, as a small and impressionable girl, to attend my Aunt Joan's wedding. Joan had once reigned as Queen of Mobile's Azalea Trail; she looked even better than royalty to me. Her storybook ceremony, along with magazine photos of Queen Elizabeth's coronation and Grace Kelly's wedding, became my guidebook for brides. My sisters and I would fill our arms with bridal wreaths or azaleas by season, and troop down the back steps, playing brides. We envisioned yards of tulle and spangly white gowns, armies of loving attendants in bright dresses. I can't speak for the others, but I never considered a groom. What would he be for?

As it happened, I was the first of us to marry. Faced with the real event, I discovered I had lost all desire for finery. I wanted to greet my husband in a simple linen dress my mother had made. I wore a lace mantilla. My father drove us to church in our International Harvester wagon, and only my sister Mary preceded me when I walked down the aisle. I realized then that all the pretending in the world hadn't prepared me for an actual wedding—nor for the apparently unavoidable prospect of entire families going mad. I had been an attendant at a wedding or two by the time my own wedding happened, but only my own family taught me the real impact of wedding insanity.

In the days before family weddings, I've begun—and broken up—more than a few arguments over (not quite) forgotten slights. I've dried tears, including my own, as we wept over nothing or everything. The night before my own wedding, my two youngest sisters came to where I stood ironing to remind me I still had the chance to make them bridesmaids. How I loved those little girls! And how I had let them down, although eventually they forgave me. Years later, when the restaurant staff didn't show for another sister's reception, the whole family, including the poor souls who had married, waited tables. We handled it so smoothly—tuxes and all—the guests thought the odd touch had been planned. Later, we chalked it up to nuptial madness.

Over the years, as my brothers and sisters strolled down their chosen aisles, our mother always approached the date with her own peculiar insanity. She was never quite prepared. Her dress needed a hem, or this bridesmaid's bodice—one of three she was making—required a small tuck. During the mayhem before every wedding, I could count on one thing: Mother would hold up an item and ask, "Would you sit down and work on this?"

By helping her, I discovered, quite by accident, a small ritual that kept me sane. While others stormed around me, I sat quietly and stitched away, shielded by Mother's unfinished projects.

But by the time my oldest son married, we lived in a world that seemed light-years from my childhood. So many traditions had changed, some beyond recognition. I considered all this as I reviewed my to-do list ahead of time and realized with sadness how much I missed my mother, prepared or not. Beyond that, I had nothing to sew.

Two days before the ceremony, I heard an unexpected knock at the door. My future daughter-in-law held up a pair of tiny blue trousers. "I know you're busy," she said, "but we need these for the ring bearer. Could you hem them, please?"

The hug I enclosed her in must have seemed extreme, but she had inadvertently rescued tradition. As I sat down to hem those small wedding clothes, I whispered a prayer for her, for us all.

Bridget Balthrop Morton

Taking the Plunge

The last time I had found myself on a tree limb hanging over water—the only other time, actually—I was fourteen years old. Then, like now, I had a decision to make. A bunch of new friends and I had gone to a local swimming hole. It was considered a right of passage to climb up this very old tree, shimmy out onto a particular limb, hang off, and let go . . . plunging into the water below.

Wanting desperately to fit in and to be accepted, I took the requisite climb. A sneaky someone followed me up the tree and blocked my path back down, in case I got cold feet. Scooting out onto the limb was easy enough; even swinging over the side into a hanging position was doable. It was the letting go part I had a hard time with. Hanging there over the water—all of my new friends' faces looking up at me expectantly—the weight of my decision bore down on me. Here was something I really wanted. Misguided motives aside, all I had to do was let go. Just trust that it would work out in the end and let go.

I hung there a little too long, I think. Every scary story my mother had ever told me about kids getting hurt doing stupid things ran through my mind. But in the end, I let go and it felt good. I took the plunge.

Now here I was, eight years later, sitting on yet another ancient tree branch, the Chattahoochee River swirling several feet below me, and the man of my dreams had just asked me to marry him.

"I wanted it to be special," he said. "Our first date was a hike in the woods."

I looked into his warm, brown eyes. "I remember. We hiked up Kennesaw Mountain." He loved everything outdoors, and I loved him. And here he was offering me all I ever wanted, total love and acceptance, a chance to put down roots and have a family of our very own.

Holding out my hand, I watched him slip the ring onto my finger and tried not to cry. "I love you," I whispered.

"I love you too," he whispered back. He pulled me closer and we kissed.

We sat there for a long while—his arms wrapped around me—content in the moment, and watched the river flow by. Yes, there would be days when life would be turbulent and murky, like the rushing water below us, but I knew the strength of our love would keep us safe above it. There would always be sunshine peeking through the leaves.

This time I hadn't hesitated, hadn't worried about getting hurt or how it would work out in the end. I took the plunge and it felt good.

Darcy Crowder

Seasons of Love

Some say that love is for the young and that it comes just once in a lifetime. But they're wrong. I know they are, because only a couple of years stood between me and my first Social Security check when I met the second great love of my life.

Call it fate. Call it the hand of God. Call it whatever you will. Sometimes wonderful things, unsought and unexpected, just happen.

Widowed at the age of forty-seven, I had learned to live alone and to like it. After twelve years, I certainly wasn't looking for love, much less marriage. But then love found me. Like a sweet fog, it crept through my defenses and swirled over the familiar landscape of my life, so slowly and softly that I didn't recognize it at first.

I was working in the church office one day, minding my own business, when my friend Kay stuck her head in the door. From the sneaky look on her face and the way she sidled up to me, I should have known she was up to something. After a little chit-chat, she nudged me. "Hey, are you seeing anyone?"

What kind of question was that? She knew as well as I that there was no one special.

Now, eyes sparkling, Kay went into full match-maker mode. "Well, would you go out to dinner with my brother?"

I remembered then that her brother Stan had lost his wife the previous winter. I've known Kay for a long time. She's a wonderful, beautiful, and vivacious person, so I figured her brother must be a pretty nice guy. "Well," I thought, "why not? It might be fun." How was I to know that the poor man was unaware of her little plot?

Not long after that, our church sponsored a dinner cruise on the Ohio River, and Kay, in her role as Cupid, brought Stan along. I first saw him standing at the railing of the sternwheeler, looking across the water to the Ohio shore with the saddest expression I had ever seen. I knew that look, having worn it myself for a long time, and my heart went out to him. Kay introduced us, and we chatted for a while. Then the boat docked, and with a wave and an "I'll see you," he was gone.

I'll see you? What did that mean? Did it mean, I'll see you—literally—or was it just another form of goodbye? After a couple of weeks, I concluded it was the latter.

Then he called. He had been out of town, and wondered if we could we have a late lunch after church on Sunday. I was surprised at the rush of excitement that enveloped me as I awaited Sunday.

It was a pleasant afternoon. He was easy to talk to. Comfortable. Before long he was making the two-hour round trip between his home in New Martinsville, West Virginia, and mine in Vienna on a regular basis. The visits became so frequent, in fact, that he often stayed overnight at his sister's—Kay's Bed and Breakfast, as we jokingly called it.

Well, that was all fine and dandy. Good company. Dinner. Plays and concerts and picnics. Phone calls that lasted into the wee hours were okay, too. But I wasn't going to get too involved. No sir. No way. Not me.

By the second Christmas we were engaged.

With a not-quite-two-year-old flower girl who ran down the aisle and jumped into Grandpa Stan's arms, and a four-year-old ring bearer so exhausted from carrying that heavy pillow that he had to lie down at the best man's feet, everyone agreed it was an interesting wedding.

At the end of the ceremony, the minister invited the immediate families to join us for a special unity prayer. And so they came—down the center aisle, down the side aisles—his kids, my kids, sons-in-law, daughters-in-law, grandkids, brothers and sisters and their spouses, every size, shape, and description, all ages from a seven-month old grandson to my eighty-two-year-old dad. We bowed our heads, and forty pairs of hands joined to form one family. Stan and I were married not only in the eyes of God, but also in the eyes of those we held most dear.

And so, on a cool Saturday in April, I stood on the steps of the Vienna Baptist Church, my new husband beside me. As I looked at my handsome husband in his tuxedo, his dark hair shot through with silver, a chilly breeze stirred the delicate fabric of my blush pink gown, and I shivered. In front of us, Bradford pear trees in full bloom lined the median on Grand Central Avenue. Traffic slowed, horns blared, and friendly folks waved as they passed. A sea of faces smiled up at us, and, as we descended, waves of cheers and applause broke around us. As scores of aqua, rose, and cream-colored balloons floated up into the uncertain spring sky, Stan squeezed my hand and winked, for we shared a wonderful secret. Together we had discovered that true love knows no season.

Patsy Evans Pittman

My War Bride

A whole new world opened up for the people of Lincolnton, Georgia, and McCormick, South Carolina, when a bridge was built over the Savannah River in 1939. These small towns, only fourteen miles apart, had never been exposed to each other. In 1941, when the road was paved on the South Carolina side, the teenagers were the first to explore. The boys from McCormick drove to Lincolnton to the West End, the local drive-in and teen hangout, to check out the new crop of girls.

It was in August that I first saw Helen Wright, the daughter of the Lincolnton mayor. She was just back from a month in Daytona Beach—tanned and beautiful—wearing a white dress in the latest style. She was only fifteen, but the prettiest little thing you ever saw. My friend, Rudolph, had dated her younger sister Vera, so on one of our many trips over the river,

I asked Rudolph to set me up with Helen. He tried, but Helen refused. She said her boyfriend had just moved away.

I kept dropping by and one day she finally went for a ride with me to keep from being rude. Helen was always busy and usually out, so I courted her mother. Mrs. Wright and I became great friends. She even helped me in my quest to see her daughter. Helen's friend Leslie also helped once, when she and Helen were on the road to McCormick. She stopped and asked Helen to get out and check the tires for a flat. As soon as Helen complied, Leslie roared off and left her stranded on the highway. Naturally, I just happened to come along to pick her up.

Helen and I dated off and on until my junior year in high school in May 1942, when I took a school deferment so I could join the Army Air Corps. My orders sent me to Maxwell Field in Montgomery, Alabama. Because I contracted double pneumonia, I was allowed to go home for two weeks in December, and by then, Helen and I were getting serious. I asked my mother to order a ring for me from the drugstore.

Helen, now a senior in high school, was a cheerleader and the class president. She was having a great time, while I was jealous, homesick, and so lonely. In February, I asked her to come to Montgomery to marry me. Both of us had to get permission from our parents, and Helen had to get the principal's approval, too.

We were married at the base chapel on February 20, 1943. Our wedding night supper was a hamburger from a filling station. We found a room at an old wooden hotel with the bathroom down the hall. Afterward, she went back to school and I went back to my base.

After Helen's graduation, my daddy gave us a 1940 Chevy Coupe, which Helen drove to Seymour, Indiana, to meet me. Shortly after Helen arrived, I received my assignment as copilot on the B-24 in Pocatello, Idaho. Since my next assignment was in Riverside, California, and I didn't want Helen driving that distance alone, I offered our car to a soldier from my unit who was on leave. He drove the car as far as North Carolina and my father picked it up from there.

In December, I was sent to San Francisco, where we would begin flying our planes across the country en route to our assignment in the war, and Helen began her return trip home by train.

With the help of a station clerk, Helen was routed to Georgia. Since it was Sunday and there was no way to verify her funds, she persuaded the ticket agent to take a personal check for $108. He trusted her but told her that if on Monday morning the check was not good, he would have her put off the train—no matter where she was.

Dressed in a suit, heels, and gloves, eighteen-year-old Helen began the journey from California to Georgia with $20 in borrowed cash, thanks to the bombardier's wife. Luckily, two businessmen and a woman took her under their wing on the first leg of the trip. They played Pokeno and the loser had to buy the meals. They made sure Helen never lost.

But when she got to her next stop, the connecting train was full of soldiers: civilians weren't allowed onboard. One soldier suggested she get on with his group, and so she did. Once on the train, Helen sat on her suitcase in the aisle, between cars, and occasionally in the lavatory with the door open. The USO served food at the stops, and the soldiers brought her something to eat each time. When she arrived in Georgia, she still had the $20 in her pocketbook!

For the next nine months, I flew my thirty missions. We wrote letters, sent pictures, and prayed. When I returned, her parents let us have their house that first night. We stayed up half the night opening wedding presents and talking. Nine months later, we were the proud parents of a baby girl. Three boys were to follow.

After sixty-two years together, Helen and I still kiss when we go over the bridge with the moonlight reflecting on the water, she still irons my underwear and our sheets, and we still call out "Pop Eye" when we pass a car with one headlight and remember the wonderful times. It was an era when two young people, so much in love, took the chance to marry during the war, and it worked. The times were such that an eighteen-year-old girl could go from coast to coast and be safely helped by so many nice people. A man of twenty-one could pilot a plane, go into combat, have his plane shot up, write a diary to the woman he loved, and come home to a wonderful future.

This little girl, whom I love very much, followed me across the country, wrote and prayed for me around the world, and is still my war bride today.

James Neal Workman, as told to Lou W. Souders

I Married My High School Sweetheart

I grew up in the old days, the days when children minded their parents and did what they were told. My mother passed away when I was quite young, so it was natural that I became very close to my father. He was all that I had, and his word was law. I didn't always agree with him, but I obeyed without question.

I wasn't allowed to date while I was in high school, but this wasn't much of a hardship because nobody asked me out, anyway. That is, until senior year.

It was a small school, and we seven graduates had become a tight little group. We all went to the prom together as a group of friends, not as individual couples.

I was allowed to go to the dance that night, and when I put on my new long gown Dad told me I was beautiful. The gym was decorated in the class colors, with lavender and white crepe paper streamers, and the lights were dimmed. It might seem corny to the teenagers of today, but for us it was a fairy kingdom and a magical night. Then to make it even more perfect, I met the handsomest boy in the whole wide world.

Bob Platt came to the gym looking for my class-mate—his sister Kate. When she introduced us and he looked at me with those blue eyes, the color of deep water, I felt as if I were drowning. Everything and everyone else faded out of existence for me.

At that time, we were experiencing the dark days of the Korean War and Bob's khaki army uniform fit like a second skin. He was a Rogers Ranger—or some other romantic title—and home on leave.

Now that I was all grown up at age seventeen, I was allowed a little more freedom. We managed to see each other almost every day for what was left of his leave. We made plans for when he would come back, and dreamed about what our life would be when he was finished making the world safe for democracy. We liked the same things. We had the same goals. We were soul mates. Admittedly, I was naïve in the ways of the world, but I was in love for the first time. And I believed in it.

The night before he was due to return to camp, he came to see me, but my father didn't think it was such a good idea to go off with him.

"I think you'd better stay home tonight," he said.

I was shocked to think I wouldn't be able to see Bob alone this one last time. But it never occurred to me to go anyway. I wanted to stomp my foot or break something, but, instead, I went to my room and cried great, racking sobs. My father came in and sat on the bed patting my shaking shoulders.

"Don't cry, honey," he said. "He'll forget all about you in six months. You'll be another girl he spent time with on leave and no more than that."

As a mature high school graduate, I wouldn't accept that. In six months my love would be back home. We'd get married, we'd get our own place, and we'd do all of the things that we had talked about.

We promised to write every day. My letters were lightly scented and on the fanciest stationery I could buy. In the long-ago days before instant mail, Bob actually did write a few letters, but they got further and further apart, until they stopped completely. Yet I waited for the postman long after I knew in my heart there would be no more letters.

I was still sure he would come back to me. After all, hadn't he declared his undying love forever? A love that would last through flood and fire? Any and every calamity?

I waited for him, planning what we would do. Would we have a big elaborate wedding, a simple ceremony, or a justice of the peace? The time for him to come home came and went, but he didn't come knocking on my door to carry me away on his metaphorical white horse. That's when I learned that you don't really die from a broken heart. You want to die or be swallowed up by a giant crocodile, but life goes on.

I heard from friends that he was seen around town with another girl. I hadn't seen his sister since graduation, so I couldn't ask her. But a person can only cry so much, and I had already shed enough tears to sink a battleship. It was time to move on. To my father's credit, he never said, "I told you so." I'm sure he thought it, though.

I went to work at a boring job. I hated it, but it kept me occupied. I needed to stay busy. I had never been a social butterfly and now I became even more of a recluse.

Several years passed and I was still comparing every man I met with Bob. I knew this was unfair and that I had not been the only girl to be left at the altar.

All of my friends were getting married, and it was time for me to stop being so picky, so I chose a young man who was as different from Bob as anyone could be. Although we didn't have much in common, I thought that love could be learned. It can't. Our differences became more pronounced as time went on.

After the divorce, I job-hopped, moving from city to city, state to state, searching for whatever it was that was missing in my life, but not quite knowing what it was.

It had been forty years since I had last seen Bob, though he was never far from my thoughts. In my mind, he was still the blue-eyed, auburn-haired twenty-year-old man I had fallen so deeply in love with.

Finally, I started asking around to see if I could find out what had happened to him. Was he married? Was he still alive? And in the midst of my questioning, I managed to obtain his phone number. I kept it for several weeks trying to decide if I should call or let the memory die. Many times I reached for the phone and stopped. What if he didn't want to meet me after all these years? But then I realized that didn't matter. What did matter was that I couldn't let it go. I needed closure.

When I finally made the call, my hands trembled. The phone rang loudly in my ear. There was a hairball in my throat, big enough to choke on, and it was hard for me to speak.

"Is Bob Platt there?" I asked, panting hard enough to be mistaken for an obscene caller.

"This is Bob."

After an agonizing moment I was able to talk.

"You might not remember me, but I'm your sister Kate's friend, Ellen. We met when you were home on leave from the service," I said stupidly, after I could catch my breath.

"I'm so glad you called! Of course I remember you. I've been looking for you for forty years! I never forgot you, but I heard you were married and happy and had a whole passel of kids. So I thought it was best to leave you alone."

He really did remember me. That first time we talked until my ear was sore.

We agreed to meet and when I finally saw him, the years disappeared like fog in the wind, and I became a teenager with sweaty palms all over again.

Three months later, in a simple ceremony, I married my high school sweetheart, forty years after our first meeting.

These days we don't spend time wondering what could have been or what should have been, we only try to make the best of the time we have now. And slowly and surely, we are finally realizing the plans we made so long ago.

Connie Vigil Platt

You Never Know

I was thirty-two years old and had an affliction. At least, that's what my grandmother and aunt decided, because I had not yet gotten married. Everyone on both sides of my family had married by the time they were twenty-four. Even both of my younger sisters were married. Thus, I was accused of being too picky, too job-oriented, too serious, and too stubborn.

The last comment came from my sixty-five-year-old aunt, who had introduced me to her friend's grandson. He was nice, but not my type. When my aunt heard that I wasn't interested, she threw her arms into the air and told my mother that I was the most stubborn girl she had ever known and that I hadn't even given this guy a chance. Of course, my mother agreed with her, and then reminisced about the last guy I had turned down because I hadn't liked his ears.

"How ridiculous is that?" Mom asked, frowning at my aunt.

When it was put like that, I had to agree. It did sound ridiculous, but I really didn't like the way his ears looked! Besides, at the moment, I had a more pressing problem: my tonsils. I was tired of being sick every winter and had decided that during Christmas vacation I would have my tonsils removed. My mother wasn't happy with this decision because it meant I couldn't accompany her to a Christmas party that her Spanish teacher was having. Fortunately, I was able to talk my sister, Patty, into going instead

After they left, I took my medication and climbed into bed. Around eleven, Patty bounded into my bedroom and shook me awake.

"Guess what?" she shouted, a huge smile on her face.

"What?" I asked, wondering if she had won the lotto.

"I met your husband-to-be!"

I jumped up and stared at her. "You did?" Was this some kind of a joke, or had my angels finally found someone for me?

"Yes! He's six feet tall, with blue eyes, and he's German. He speaks four languages just like his mother. Oh, and he majored in chemistry with a minor in geology from the University of Chicago!"

"Wow!" I said. "When can I meet him?"

"Well, there is a bit of a problem."

"A problem?"

"Kind of. He lives a little south from here," she said, still trying to remain excited.

"How far south does he live?"

"Some distance . . . south," Patty replied.

"Really?" I asked. I could feel my disappointment mounting. "You mean like in Georgia?"

"No, a little farther than that."

"Oh, great, then, Mexico? Or Brazil?"

"Actually, a little farther."

"What!" I yelled, and then grabbed my throat as the pain of raising my voice registered. I glared at her, then whispered, "You woke me up to tell me my husband-to-be is in . . . in . . . Where is he?"

"Don't get mad. He's in Montevideo, Uruguay, but he does come up every Christmas for six to eight days."

I half laughed at her serious face. "Gee, too bad I missed him this Christmas. But let's hope I can meet him next Christmas, and then maybe if we're lucky we can get to know each other in five to six years." By this time, my throat throbbed with pain. "I can't believe you woke me up to tell me about a guy who lives in Uruguay!"

"But I really think that you two are meant to be," she said softly.

"A guy who lives over 7,000 miles away—and comes up once a year—is going to meet me and ask me to marry him?"

"I know it sounds a little far-fetched," Patty said helplessly, "but I believe that you two are meant to be. I'm truly sorry that I woke you." She helped me snuggle back into the bed. "Get some sleep. I'll call you tomorrow."

After Patty left, I lay there thinking how stupid the idea was. It was simply ridiculous.

But life is crazy and, as it turned out, I was wrong. The following Christmas, Hans and I met and ended up spending the entire eight days together. After he left, my mother couldn't help but tease me, asking if I was okay with his ears. This time I had to smile. If there was a problem with his ears, I certainly hadn't noticed.

He came back that summer and we spent ten more days together. Two years from the time my sister said she had met my husband-to-be, he proposed marriage.

On my wedding day, my grandfather smiled at me and nodded toward my new husband. "You took a while to find your guy, but only eighteen days to know he was the one."

A slow smile spread across my face. I hadn't looked at it that way, but Grandfather was right. Almost from the minute I saw him, I knew he was the one I had been waiting for.

Linda Lipscomb Juergensen

Huckleberry Romance

The fabric of Pauline's blue robe glistens in the morning sun as she passes by the window. Quietly she places a glass of orange juice in front of me and then slips gracefully into her chair so that we are face-to-face at the breakfast table. She raises those big brown eyes of hers and studies my face.

"Where do we go from here, Harold? How are we going to do this?"

I smile. "I guess we start at the beginning."

"Can you remember that far back?" she asks, returning the smile.

I laugh out loud at her remark. "Sure I can. I remember what happened in 1931 better than what I did yesterday!"

The mission we are on today will require that memory, for our two daughters have been after us for years to put the story of our romance down on paper. They want every last detail for posterity, and we have finally succumbed.

"I think we should start at the huckleberry patch," I say.

My sweetheart shakes her head. "But that wasn't the first time I saw you. It was at the Gilboa School prom. You asked Opal's date if you could dance with her, and she came back and told me that I should dance with Harold Hackley." Pauline frowns. "But you never asked my date if you could!"

I have been married long enough to know to choose my words carefully, so without missing a beat, I reply. "Honey, I couldn't risk showing the prettiest girl and best dancer in the area my lack of skill."

Pauline rolls her eyes and smacks my hand playfully. "Do you want to write this, or shall I?" She reaches across the table to the pen and paper. "It was July 28, 1931, and raining, so you couldn't work in the fields . . . "

I pick up where she left off. "Dad called Mr. Wagner for permission to pick in his berry patch." I wiggle my eyebrows up and down suggestively. "That sounded good to me—I got out of the hot fields and maybe I could get a glimpse of Mr. Wagner's good-looking daughter."

Pauline glances up from the paper. "You ornery thing!"

I wink and keep on talking. "There were six of us—and hordes of mosquitoes—picking in your woods that day. After a while, three of us young folks got very thirsty and came up to get a drink from the old hand pump." I pause and let the memory roll over me. "Remember how we had to prime those things, then pump like mad?" Pauline nods, the pen gliding over the paper.

"While we were trying to retrieve some water, we heard this sweet voice calling from the house. I turned around and there on the porch stood this beautiful dark-haired girl." I smile widely and lean forward. "Do you remember what you said to us?"

Pauline frowns. "I think I asked you about the picking or something like that, but what I do remember is that you broke some kind of speed record getting to that porch!"

Pauline is right. I was not about to pass up an opportunity like that! I don't recall what we said to each other, either, but I remember that I had plans—that would not be the last time I would chat with the beautiful dark-haired girl. The moment I left her porch, my buddy and I hopped into my '28 Chevy and beat it to Remington so I could find a phone, call that beautiful dark-haired girl, and make a date for that same night.

My mind whirled with sweet memories. The double-date with Opal and Ernie. Riding around town.

"If memory serves, we didn't go to a movie or dinner." I say with a smile.

From across the table, Pauline grins. "I was happy just to be with you."

"On our second date, I proposed!" I shake my head at the urgency of youth.

Pauline's smile grows soft as she takes up the pen again and begins writing. "How much detail should we volunteer?"

My eyebrows rise emphatically. "I think we should leave a lot to their imaginations."

With that remark, it is Pauline's turn to chuckle. She taps the pen on the table gently to get my attention. "I should tell them that—since I was in charge of securing the band for my junior prom—you and I got to lead the Grand March." A faraway look sparkles in her eyes for a moment and then a soft sigh escapes. "I wore an aqua ankle-length dress with crystal jewelry."

In an instant, I am enveloped in a vision of her in that dress and I am moved. "You looked almost as snazzy that night as the night you got married in it," I say and mean it.

"Thank you, dear," she says, and then coyly looks down at the tablet she's been writing on. "But I seem to recall that you were none too happy about my having to scout that band. Something about a dinner dance in Chicago with someone else..."

I pretend to bristle, but instead my mind whirls off in another direction. Had Pauline ever figured out why she got her engagement ring so soon after that trip? The way I saw it, I had no choice. I had to let the male population know she was out of circulation. The ring—a third of a carat purchased from Montgomery Ward—set me back thirty bucks.

Back then, we had our song, and we also had our tree—a huge willow tree in an old schoolyard. On my birthday, April 12, 1934, I proposed to my dark-haired beauty under the spreading boughs of our tree. The best gift I ever received was hearing her say, "Oh, Harold. Yes!"

These were hard times for everyone during the Depression, so rather than having a big wedding we eloped three months later on July 28, 1934. The date was exactly three years from the day we had met on Pauline's porch steps. I will always remember it as the day I went to pick huckleberries and found a peach, instead.

As that thought enters my mind, I turn and gaze at Pauline's smiling face. I smile back. My peach is just as sweet today as she was seventy years ago.

Harold and Pauline Hackley, as
told to Barbara K. Williams

A God Thing

I might have pinched myself, had I not needed both hands to hold the large bouquet of sweet peas and baby's breath. It could have been a dream, it was so . . . I searched for the correct word, but one word wouldn't do. "It's a God thing," I thought, and a smile came to my face. There we were, in rural Colorado, standing beneath an arch in a barn, preparing to utter the famous words: "I do." As the pastor talked about the sanctity of marriage, it was as if I heard him through a wall of fog.

Turning to look at my intended, my heart leapt. How could this tall, handsome cowboy want to marry me? This wonderful man, who had lost two previous wives to cancer, now smiled down at me adoringly. God must have known I needed someone like him, for how else had he landed in my life? For him to have found me, just when he did, had to be some kind of miracle.

I had been a mess, to say the least, and still reeling from several very harsh realities. As my sixtieth birthday approached, my husband of thirty years had suddenly left me for a younger woman. That shock was followed closely by another devastating blow: the death of my dear mother far away in England. With the help of friends, I got to Europe for the funeral. I certainly hadn't expected that another leap of faith would be needed before I returned home, but it was. Forty-eight hours after my arrival in England, my daughter called to tell me that my home had been badly damaged by a tornado. I accepted the news calmly, which frightened my sister. She felt sure I was in shock. But it was God's grace that gave me peace and made me realize I was 6,500 miles away—there was nothing I could do to change what had happened; so, instead, I accepted it.

Returning to the United States two weeks later, I discovered that a wonderful team of volunteers had cleaned up what must have been a horrendous mess on my property. It still looked scary to me, but photographs taken by a friend showed the enormous amount of cleanup that had already taken place.

It turned out that the man who had done the most work was the friend of one of my neighbors. He had traveled nearly thirty miles with his tractor, chain saw, and other needed tools and had organized the volunteers into teams. Together they removed the trees that had toppled against the house, moved heavy appliances and other debris, and cleared a path so the damage control team could enter the premises. It was this man who made my home temporarily livable, and he didn't even know me!

When I finally tracked him down to thank him for his hard work, I found a gentle, humble man who made light of his labors. Although his bright blue eyes immediately caught my attention, I was cautious. I couldn't run the risk of being hurt again.

But despite the hard work, it was clear my property would never be the same. The tornado had shifted the old foundation. Floors sagged, windows had cracked and shattered, and cupboard doors no longer shut. If the house couldn't be saved, the property would have to be sold.

But before it could be sold, the land would have to be cleared. The pasture in front of the house still bore witness to the tornado, and with so much debris, it resembled a landfill. There were glass, bricks, paper and pencils, and tree limbs everywhere, and the front half of the High School, which had originally been located opposite my property, now was lying in my horse pasture.

Al Cook, my handsome knight, rode in on his John Deere tractor every day—until the property was presentable again.

One afternoon, as we sat on the porch drinking lemonade, I mentioned that my feet were tired from standing at the ironing board.

"Take off your shoes and put your feet in my lap," Al said, with a flash of his blue eyes. At first I hesitated. It had to be those eyes, for in the next second I was putting my feet into his strong capable hands. As he began his magic, a big smile lit his face.

"Hold on," he said. "I'm going to melt you right into that chair." And he did.

Today, as I stand in Al's barn, I look around at the colorful antique quilts that decorate the walls and the strands of twinkling white lights that sparkle along the wooden beams, and I feel the warmth—old-fashioned, welcoming warmth. The country band—squeezed into the 1800s chuck wagon—is poised, ready to play, and friends and neighbors sit around on bales of hay, waiting for me to say "I do."

Later someone said it was exactly five o'clock when I said the words. They knew because Grinder, the old ranch horse, who had been turned out of his stall to accommodate troughs of iced soda, had made his entrance at just that moment. Shoving his head in through the open barn door, he had let out a loud whinny. Al says it was because Grinder was always fed at five and was looking for his supper, but I like to think he was giving his approval.

Cariad Rhys-Cook

Come, Grow Old with Me

There's something ominous about your fortieth birthday. It marks the entrance into middle age. No longer is your whole life before you. The realization dawns that you will not live forever and that youthful sense of invincibility disappears beyond the horizon.

My fortieth birthday was celebrated festively. My friends gathered at a local restaurant—the men wore black armbands, the women out-of-style black hats with veils. They were in mourning for my passing into middle age. My gifts included an assortment of old-age aids such as hemorrhoid ointment, a cane with a horn and a rearview mirror, pill boxes, and an abundance of funeral literature. They even tried unsuccessfully to rent a hearse.

I took the teasing in stride and laughed at the outlandishness, but when they all went home and I climbed into bed that night, I was left with an emptiness that surprised me. Their jokes didn't seem so funny anymore. They were too close to the truth: I was over the hill. My life was perhaps half over.

As the months passed, I became more and more aware of aches and pains, more aware of my limitations. I could no longer race the kids to the mailbox without becoming winded. I couldn't touch my toes anymore, either, and tennis was not nearly as inviting.

"Old age sure isn't for sissies," I complained to my husband, Ted.

He looked at me with a puzzled frown. "What do you mean? We're not old."

"Well, I sure feel old."

"Well, you don't look it." He smiled and kissed me on the top of my head. It was a nice compliment, but I felt dismissed. He wasn't taking me seriously. Didn't he realize we were, if not yet old, at least getting very close to it?

Imperceptibly, my attitude changed and I wondered what these heretofore unnoticed symptoms might mean. My trips to the doctor's office became more frequent, though I suspected he wasn't taking me seriously, either. I read up on different diseases and began to self-diagnose. I was sure my indigestion was a heart attack, my headache a cerebral hemorrhage, which had been the cause of my mother's death. I hated the hypochondriac I had become, but I seemed held in bondage by my fears.

"Why don't you get a thorough physical by a different doctor, get a fresh perspective?" Ted suggested after I had taken several days in succession off work despite the fact that my family doctor had pronounced me healthy.

"Yes," I agreed. "I'm sure Dr. Jones missed something."

But the internist concurred with my family practitioner and suggested I might be depressed and that perhaps I should go for counseling. I was embarrassed to tell Ted nothing was wrong, and I was embarrassed to go to a counselor. More than being depressed, I felt fearful, a cold hard knot in the pit of my stomach that said something was wrong and if they didn't find it, death was hovering at my door. In my mind, I realized these fears were unfounded—silly, even—but I could not shake the overwhelming sense of doom.

This was the sad state I had come to, although even today, I cannot trace all the steps I took to get there. I felt isolated. No one, not even Ted, understood how I felt, or so I thought.

My forty-first birthday was coming up.

"How about having a few friends over?" Ted suggested.

"I don't think so," I said, shaking my head. "I'm not up to it." My glumness had settled over us like a funeral pall. Ted's hopeful smile crumbled.

The morning of my birthday dawned, bright and clear. But instead of embracing the day, I pulled the covers up over my head. I didn't want to face another year older and deeper in fear.

"Oh no, you don't," Ted said as he gently tugged at the blanket. "I've got a birthday surprise for you."

"I don't like surprises," I grumbled, but my head slowly emerged. Ted sat cross-legged on the bed, patiently waiting for me to come out of hibernation. In his hands was a gaily wrapped box, about a foot square.

"I hope you like it."

As I struggled with the tape, he warned, "Be careful. It's breakable."

Gingerly, I pulled a delicate and fragile statue of a very old couple from the package. Both were bent over. The woman was leaning on the man; the man was leaning on a cane. Their faces were lined and wrinkled, but it was their eyes that drew my attention. Years of tenderness were reflected, their love evident.

Ted leaned toward me and stroked my face. His love-filled eyes intently probed mine. "That's us! We're going to grow old together. Let loose of that terrible fear you have, Sweetheart." Then borrowing a line from Robert Browning, he added "Come, grow old along with me, the best is yet to be."

That was some twenty-five years ago. I have grown old with Ted. That moment was the beginning of healing for me, the breaking of the chains of fear that bound me. In that one pristine moment it all became clear to me. Ted did know how I was feeling! He understood what I was going through and wanted me to know he would always be there for me to lean on, as I would be there for him to lean on. And that—in a nutshell—is what love and marriage is all about.

For Ted and me, the best really is yet to be.

Nancy Baker

Happily Ever After

At the age of thirty-four, a divorced mother of three, I lived in a house on a mountain right outside Cartersville, Georgia, where I aspired to write. Writing filled those lonely cracks, masking them as solitude. In my spare time, I attended a local writing group, passed cold nights with good books, and in the warm season tended my herb garden. Sometimes a thought moved through my mind like a wisp of smoke: I'd like to meet a good man, maybe go to a movie or dinner. But, mostly, I had resigned myself to a full life that was, and I thought would remain, devoid of marriage.

Like many well-planned lives, however, one day my plans were thrown to the wind. I never went out, but on the spur of the moment, I agreed to attend my brother's birthday party at a local establishment. As I put on my makeup that evening, an odd sense of excitement fluttered in my stomach like butterfly wings, as if some elusive figure waited just outside my reach.

Holding my head high, I drove down the mountain dressed to kill. I refused to look like the poor divorced sister. The scene I encountered when I arrived was just what I had pictured: smoke, drinks, and loud music. What was I doing here? As the crowd warmed up, I pulled on my coat.

Turning to go, I couldn't help but notice a man with remarkable blue eyes sitting at the table across from me. I looked away when I realized he was returning my stare. But something in that stare made the butterflies come to life again. Maybe I would stay for one more song. I dipped my head and nervously sipped my diet soda.

"Excuse me, Miss," said a male voice at my elbow. Startled, I looked up. The man with the remarkable blue eyes was now standing in front of me. Pleasantly surprised, I looked into those eyes.

"Yes?" I asked.

"My name is Jack," he said, holding out his hand. I looked at his hand for a moment before I accepted it. A handshake? Did it get better?

"Ann," I replied.

"Ann, would you like to dance?"

I shook my head slightly.

Jack spoke faster. "Please don't say no. I feel so out of place sitting here. I came with my brother for a friend's birthday. I don't go out much. I'm not much on dancing. Let's just pretend we're having a good time. Okay?"

I softened, just a bit. "Okay," I said. Okay? What? What had I just agreed to?

The rock music required real dancing, not just a shuffling of feet, and after three songs my joints had loosened like the hinges of a freshly oiled door. As the music turned slow, it seemed natural to dance close, so I moved into Jack's arms.

One slow dance led to a real date. One date turned into three months of dates. My girls liked him, and Jack's son liked me. Life was complete. I had someone to cook for on the weekends, someone to share my thoughts with at night. The precious first three months turned into a year, and we celebrated by returning to the place where we had met. We danced slow and close, and love sparked. And a year turned into a long-term relationship. I didn't think life could get any better.

Exactly four years later, on a Saturday night, I heard a knock at my door. I opened the door to find Jack, dressed in a black suit and tie, holding a dozen roses. My daughters stood behind me smiling like proud mothers, while Jack knelt down on one knee, and the room spun about wildly.

"I love you, Ann," Jack said, his voice full of emotion. "Will you marry me?"

All those plans of living a nice life alone escaped in one word. "Yes," I whispered.

Six months later, on May 3, 1997, we were married in a full-blown wedding, created and directed by my daughters. And, if, at that moment, I had thought that life couldn't get any better, I would have been wrong. Two years later, I gave birth to a little girl, Ella, who had her daddy's incredible eyes.

Two families had merged to become one. To this day, through all the chaos a blended family can bring, when I look into Jack's eyes, I still get goose bumps and I know where I belong.

Ann Hite

The Getaway

I t was a long six years to live with a stepmother. Only seven when her mother died, Mahetable never forgot that day, and how the horses drew the coffin on a sled through a blizzard to the burial ground.

For three years, Hettie, as she was called, helped her older sister Mary manage the household, while their older brothers assisted their father. When their father remarried a widow with three children, he brought them all to live at the farm. Soon, Mary left home as a bride, and Hettie was left to cope with: "Hettie! Fetch in another load o' kindlin'," and "Hettie, them taters needs peelin'." And so it went.

Hettie met Ed Stephens on May 26, 1850—the day her brother Jacob married Jane Miley. Although they were immediately attracted to one another, Hettie was only fourteen and her father and stepmother discouraged the relationship. Ed still came calling on Sundays after church services, but the elders saw to it that the two were never alone for more than a few minutes.

Not long after her fifteenth birthday, Hettie walked Ed to where his horse, Nellie, was hitched. "Hettie, you're fifteen now. You said your ma was but fifteen when she wedded up with your pap—he bein' twenty-one. Me, I'm twenty-two. D'ya think I could speak to your pap?"

Hettie shook her head. "Pap told me she was too young. Havin' all those babies too soon. Said twenty plenty soon enough. Eighteen at the leastest." She looked up at him, at the veil of sadness in his eyes. "Oh, Ed, I wish . . . "

Ed's mouth came down on hers for a moment only, before she tore herself away. She stood by quietly as he mounted his horse, and then looked down at her. "I ain't waitin' no three years for you, Hettie. Not fer Pap. Not fer nobody. I guarantee it."

Though she was oppressed and overworked, Hettie could not always restrain her high spirits and mischievous nature. One day, aggravated by her lazy stepsister's neglect of egg-gathering, Hettie, coming from the direction of the chicken coop, picked up the corners of her apron and breezed by her stepmother, who sat on the porch. She sailed along, head high, pigtails gleaming like copper in the sun, smiling to herself.

"Hettie! What've you got there?"

"Nothin'. Ain't got nothin'!"

Her stepmother glared at her. "Come back here. Let me see."

Hettie stopped, turned toward her stepmother, and dropped her apron. Her stepmother—fully expecting to see eggs come tumbling out—gasped. But nothing of the sort happened because Hettie had told the truth. The apron was empty.

Her stepmother pointed a finger at her and declared, "Your father will hear about this, Miss Sassy Pants!"

That night after supper, armed with a switch, her father took her outside, questioned her, and then directed her to hold out her hands for punishment. She held her hands out and shut her eyes, bracing for the first sting of the switch. When nothing happened, she opened her eyes and saw her father gazing at her reddened, rough calloused hands.

"No more aggravation, then, hear?" he mumbled as he tossed away the switch.

When Hettie's older brother Jacob—her rock and comfort—took his wife and moved away, she turned to her brother Will for support. When Will left for the California gold mines in January of 1852, Hettie's last consoling straw went with him.

The birth of a new stepbrother added to her workload and helped her make up her mind. She met with Ed in a secret rendezvous in a field some distance from the house. Hettie stepped away from Ed's embrace and leaned against a tree.

"How long, Hettie?" he asked, again. "How long?"

"That's what I come to tell you," she explained, choosing her words carefully. "Told Pap I'd wait. Didn't say how long. I'll be sixteen next birthday, March 22."

The morning of March 21, as soon as she could slip away, Hettie gathered a few of her sparse belongings, tied them in a shawl, and dropped them from an upstairs window. She then retrieved the bundle, and concealed it in the straw near the barn. That night, she tucked the baby into his cradle and tip-toed carefully from the room. As she came near the bedroom door, she nearly collided with her father.

She hesitantly touched his arm. He looked at her, eyebrows raised. His eyes, blue like her own, but faded, shone in the candlelight. Hettie shook her head. "Nothin'. G'night, Pap."

She went into her room, pulled her nighty on over her dress, and slipped into bed beside her step-sisters. When she heard their deep-sleep breathing, she eased out of bed, took off her nighty, and looked out the window.

There, below her, she made out two shadowy figures. Hettie crept out of the window and lowered herself into Ed's waiting arms. He lifted her onto Nellie and seated himself in front. She threw her arms about his waist and pressed her body against his as he guided the horse toward the barn.

At the barn, she slid off the horse and picked up her parcel. She knelt beside Joe, the old collie, and put her arms around his neck. "G'bye, Joe. G'bye, boy."

Ed helped her up again, dug his heels into the horse's flanks, and guided the horse toward Senecaville and freedom. In Senecaville, two men emerged from a tavern, just as the pair galloped by on their way to the preacher.

"Lordamercy on us! See what I jest seen? 'Peared like a passel o' Injuns was after 'em!"

"More'n likely was the old Harry, the devil hisself, a-nippin' at their heels."

After their wedding, Mahetable and Ed settled on a farm in Illinois, where they prospered and multiplied, rearing eight children. Hettie was no stranger to hard work and large families, but this time around it was everything she had expected and hoped it would be.

Mary Helen Straker

Embedded Bliss

Of all the things a long-time married couple can do to test their love, buying a new bed is, in my estimation, number one on the list.

For more than thirty years, my husband Tom and I have shared a double bed, which I'd purchased from a coworker for $35 prior to our marriage. The bed had a new mattress but the box spring was older—much older—judging by the faded fabric of blue cabbage roses and lack of webbing.

Because a bed brings the most baggage with it, and is a place of intimacy where all of life's most interesting events take place, a married couple should, I suppose, start out fresh. But in our case, whatever ghosts haunted our used bed's sturdy springs managed to serve us and our dogs well over the years—first accommodating a heavyset beagle blend, who snored on top of the covers, and then a miniature schnauzer, who tunneled beneath the blankets to hyperventilate at our feet.

Over the years, we bought several new mattresses. Each time, we exulted in the firmness. But eventually the inevitable occurred, and our bodies rolled together in the center.

Aside from weight gain, we have experienced our share of medical issues and have slept in the same bed in sickness as well as in health. Though it is difficult to share a bed with twenty-five staples in your abdomen, it can be done. It can also be done with hives, head colds, pungent muscle ointments, and even spastic leg cramps.

But did it always have to be "until death do us part"?

That was the question we faced when we became motivated to purchase a brand new bed. We had initially ordered a new box spring and mattress but soon discovered that the metal frame on our bed was too short to support them properly.

I envisioned the years to come: both of us lowering our creaking bodies into the narrow confines of a double bed, kicking more and more feebly to claim our own space. Of course, we could always move to separate rooms, but that wasn't at all appealing. Or we could opt for twin beds. But there was something maidenly and spinsterish about such an arrangement, as if, like Henry the VIII, we could suddenly pretend after years of marriage that we had never been married at all.

"Maybe we should buy a king," I suggested, tempted by fond memories of the football field–size beds we had shared while traveling.

Tom shook his head. "Too lonely."

I was touched. "Queen, then," I said, as I watched the man I love systematically check out the next row of mattresses. Joining him, we measured the queen-size beds and learned that there was only a six-inch difference between a double and a queen. Our eyes met over the measuring tape. Six inches of additional space was not enough of a span to impress either of us. Tom's gaze moved to the next stack of mattresses and then back to me.

I smiled. "Double it is."

As for the bed frame itself, we chose a headboard and a footboard of solid pine, stained a warm honey color. The mattress rested on a box spring so high up from the floor that when I sat on it, I could actually dangle my feet. What really sold me on the bed, though, were the bedposts: four little balls with flattened tops.

At first, I couldn't think of what the bedposts reminded me of, but I knew it was something good. Finally, I put my finger on it, and had to laugh. That simple design conjured up the slightly worn eraser end of a classic No. 2 pencil, a symbol of how we'd met. We were hired as cub reporters for a daily news-paper back when a notepad was made of paper, a laptop was where you put the notepad to write in it, and your editor's tool of choice was a pencil.

As we left the store that day, I think we both realized that no matter how our bodies may age and how our sleep patterns may vary, our love is what gives us sweet dreams.

Nan B. Clark

Curfews and Credit Cards

In 1954, college dormitories still had curfews and housemothers, matriculation lost out to matrimony for many coeds, and credit cards hadn't been invented yet. Against this cultural backdrop, I packed my tennis racket and my wardrobe and set out for Central Washington College of Education. Now it is a full-fledged university; then, it was "Sweecy," an excellent place to become a teacher of English.

Today, strolling up Eighth Avenue in Ellensburg, Washington, it is easy to remember things as they were. The old brick buildings still grace the green knoll on the north side of the avenue, as do the administration building, whose stately spire once had not threatened to topple, the library, and the auditorium where we watched ten-cent movies and music recitals. On the other side of the street, Munson Hall still stands, dark-stoned and dignified, dwarfed by the modern high-rise that now houses men and women alike.

Today's sophisticated young college woman would deem 1950s dorm life quaint. We thought so, too, but no amount of complaining changed anything. The rooms of Munson Hall were occupied by girls, and girls only. Upon the infrequent occasion when a male might be permitted past the double doors, he was heralded with the loud warning, "Man on the floor!" My father dreaded helping me cart my belongings up to the third floor.

The doors were locked at the witching hour, and if a girl was left outside, she had to ring the bell for the ever-vigilant housemother. That resulted in certain grounding, but staying out the rest of the night resulted in certain expulsion.

In spite of the curfew, romance flourished, and as the year drew to a close we were often called to the large parlor to celebrate an engagement. We would encircle the bride-to-be and harmonize "I love you truly, truly, dear." Then we would file by for a close look at the ring, squeal our admiration, and hug the lucky girl. I added my squeals, but love and marriage were not part of my own itinerary. I was headed down a different track. My destination was a degree.

My derailment came in the form of a blond-haired, blue-eyed transfer student from Oregon. The first meeting did not go well. He was sprawled the length of a couch in the student union building, where we students went to pick up our mail, buy food and beverages, and bird-dog. When he and I were introduced, he failed to stand up. Manners counted in those days.

The next day, he caught my eye in the student union cafeteria. Upright, he was quite handsome. He guided me to a booth and asked if he could buy me a cup of coffee. "That would be nice," I said, forgetting for the moment that he'd been rude and that I hated coffee.

Casual conversation followed, and then he asked, "Would you be willing to go to the dime movie with me on Saturday?" A hint of a smile suggested he already knew the answer. "And by the way," he added. "I apologize for my behavior last night. I'm usually not such a clod."

Soon we were constant companions—within curfew limits, of course—and before we knew it, a year had flown by. It was customary to go steady, but Dean and I never saw the need to formalize our relationship with anything as silly as my wearing his letterman's jacket or hanging his class ring on a chain around my neck.

Then spring melted the ice and warmed the sap of the greening trees that dotted the college campus. In a surprise turn of events, Dean invited a comely wench named Rhonda to opening night of the drive-in movie. I signaled my displeasure by smashing a wooden chair into its component parts in the cafeteria. We refer to it as the time we broke up forever and ever for two weeks. I could hardly bear to leave my dorm room. My grades suffered. Dean later confessed that he, too, was miserable, and his parents, whom I'd grown to love, wouldn't talk to him.

One afternoon Dean was waiting outside the door as I left my Victorian Prose class. "Would you like a ride to work?" he asked.

"I suppose," I said, keeping my face in neutral, controlling the internal shivers that were threatening to make me chatter in the warm sunshine. We walked to his car in silence.

"You'll be early," he said, knowing my schedule. "Do you mind running by Button Jewelers?"

"That would be fine," I replied. His dad repaired watches for Mr. and Mrs. Button. We had picked up and delivered work often. He parked and walked around to open my door. I took his offered hand, and the current between us nearly lifted me off of my feet.

Mrs. Button smiled broadly when she saw us, and she set down the tray of earrings she was showing a customer. "I'll get it," she said and disappeared through the open vault door. I waited at the counter with Dean, wishing I could link my arm through his in our old, comfortable way. Mrs. Button returned with Mr. Button in tow and a small felt box, not the usual manila envelope full of broken watches.

Without warning, Dean turned to me, opened the box and exposed a sparkling diamond ring. "Will you marry me?" he asked. His eyes were solemn, but the hint of smile gave him away; he already knew the answer.

Customers gathered around us. Mrs. Button cried. Mr. Button pumped Dean's hand. It was so much better than "I love you truly" in off-pitch harmony.

The Buttons were fine people, given to charitable works. But they were in business, and credit cards were a thing of the future. The ring stayed in the vault until it was fully paid for, and my dorm sisters had to traipse off with me to the jewelry store to squeal their admiration.

Although that was 1956, some things just don't change; the ring is still on my finger, young people still bird-dog in the union building, and Button Jewelers still sits on the corner of Fourth and Pine.

Dorothy Read

A Time to Treasure

"I don't need to carry something old in our wedding, because I've got you, my octogenarian hunk," I said to my fiancé.

"And we are both starting a new life, so all we need is something borrowed and something blue," he replied.

We were acting like a couple of giggly teenagers instead of two old, widowed gray-hairs as we planned our secret wedding.

I had been alone now for ten years following my husband's death, and he and I had been together for forty years. Bruce had been married twice and had outlived both of his wives. When Bruce had been the pastor of our church, my husband and I and Bruce and his wife, Rosa Lee, had been friends. When Bruce and Rosa Lee left the state, we lost track of each other until Bruce came back to preach a revival at that same church.

When our paths crossed again, I learned that Rosa Lee, too, had passed away. That's when Bruce asked if he could correspond with me. This progressed to visiting, and finally we decided to marry. Just once, we discussed the advisability of marrying at our advanced age.

But I had already made up my mind. I looked into his eyes and told him exactly how I felt. "One day with you is worth more to me than years with a lesser man. Let's go for it," I said.

The vows were to be traditional, but I prevailed on the preacher in secret to add one additional vow to the end of the other "I do's." Bruce got a taste of what he was in for with me when the preacher asked, "Wanda, do you promise to laugh at all your husband's jokes, no matter how bad they are or how many times you have heard them, until death do you part?"

Keeping a straight face, I replied, "I do."

My first day in my new home was filled with memories. Bruce's kitchen range had knobs that turned on and off opposite to mine, so our first meal was filled with smoke alarms and laughter.

Later that day, I tried out riding his lawn mower while he caught up on some work in his home office. I soon discovered the turning radius was different than on mine back home. In no time, I had run it up a 4 × 4 bird feeder pole before I was able to stop.

Filled with trepidation, I went inside to inform my new husband. I expected fireworks but instead was met with another fit of laughter.

"Oh, wait until I tell everyone about your first day here," he said.

Everything was new and funny and beautiful to us.

As soon as we could plan it, we had a family gathering so I could meet my three new stepdaughters, their seven children and spouses, plus Bruce's sixteen great-grandchildren. I had no idea how I would be received. I shouldn't have worried. Because they saw that Bruce was not sad anymore, they welcomed me. The children showered me with bouquets of blooming weeds, and a celebration for my coming birthday was planned that day.

Once the family found out I had started digging a hole for a water garden, I was in for a surprise. A few days later, on a holiday weekend, the family arrived with picks, shovels, a pickup load of rocks and gravel, and wheelbarrows, and even the children brought little pails and shovels. The water garden, complete with a small waterfall, was finished by the end of the day. We were all dirty and exhausted, but our happiness shows in the picture I took beside the new pond.

Bruce and I were happier than we had been in many years. Then suddenly he developed a chronic cough, and when the doctor's tests came back, it was not good. He had the same type of cancer that had taken his second wife, Rosa Lee, and it was inoperable.

One day, as I was helping him dress, he looked at me, his eyes full of remorse. "I would never have gotten you into this if I had known, but I do not know what I would do without you."

I put my arms around him. "The time we have together is something to treasure forever. I'm thankful I'm here to be with you through this. No regrets!"

He died before our second anniversary.

In the years since he left us, his family and I have grown closer. I'm still GW, for Grandma Wanda, to the great-grandkids, and life goes on, despite our great loss. But I try not to complain. After all, God gave me a special treasure to cherish until I, too, leave this world: our beautiful memories together and a wonderful family to love.

Wanda Huffstutter

Small Packages of Love

I learned firsthand, during the summer of 1955, what love at first sight was all about. I had just graduated from Moline Senior High School, and it looked, boy-wise, like a dismal summer ahead—until my church group girlfriends and I discovered a group of boys at another local church. We wasted no time in inviting them to a Singspiration—an evening of singing and fellowship. They accepted.

Later, several of us drove by the house slowly where the two groups were to meet. We didn't notice any unfamiliar cars and had decided to drive on past when someone saw us, yelled out an open window, and encouraged us to come in. It was one of the smartest moves I've ever made, for there was Don among the visiting guys, and right there on the spot Cupid's arrow found its mark.

Don drove me home that evening and invited me to go swimming at Lake Story, which is a park about forty-five miles from Moline. But traveling that distance for a first date with a boy I hardly knew was (understandably) enough to make my parents hesitate. Fortunately the neighbors were customers of a Moline drugstore owned by Don's father, George. They came to my rescue, assuring my parents that George was a fine man. That was good enough for Mom and Dad.

The day dawned sunny and warm—perfect for spending time with a favorite beau. Unfortunately, I came home with a serious sunburn, and to say my father was unhappy would have been the understatement of the year. Don raced out the back door. I was so upset that I refused to speak to my father for several days.

Then a package arrived in our mailbox: a bottle of suntan lotion from the drugstore. Next came the call from Don. Later that year, on our very first Christmas as a couple, Don's gift to me was a pair of Roman Stripe nylons, complete with seams, vintage 1955. They were a huge disappointment.

Don redeemed himself on Christmas Eve the following year. Christmas filled every corner of my house. Don took my hand and led me from room to room. My heartbeat quickened as I wondered what he was doing, and I soon found out. When he failed to find a place where we could talk in private, he opened the last door that remained closed—the bathroom door—and a high-pitched scream greeted us. There sat my Aunt Thyra Maria Susanna, her peach-colored bloomers lying at her feet. Deflated, Don slammed the door, turned to me, and said "here," and without another word, shoved a blue velvet box with a sparkling diamond into my hands. It was hardly romantic, but that didn't stop me from accepting the surprise package of love.

Three years after the Singspiration of 1955, wedding bells rang for four young couples. All were romances that had begun on the eve of what we felt would be a dismal summer. We couldn't have been more wrong.

In 1998, Don surprised me again with a beautifully wrapped package. This time he had arranged a dinner party for our anniversary and presented the gift to me after the renewal of our vows. Inside was a delicate ruby and diamond bracelet that I will always cherish. We were not alone this time, either, but at least this time there was romance in the air!

Sharon Kingan Young

A Blonde and a Boy Scout

I looked up at my mother hopefully. "He seems real nice. I know we've only been going out a few weeks, but I like him a lot. He's different from most of the guys I've dated."

In the seven years since my divorce, every man I'd dated was a poster boy for America's Most Not Wanted list of men. I had finally given up. Demoralized, and tired of raising three kids on my own, I had moved into the redneck community of farmers and shoe factory workers where my parents now lived.

"I'm glad to be close to you and Dad," I said honestly, "but I doubt I'll find a husband here. It's time I relied on my own smarts to make a home and a life for my children."

Mom shushed me with a stern look. "Don't be so quick to give up. You'll find someone."

When? I wondered. When I was so old, it wouldn't matter? In my quest to find my own niche, I joined a softball team. It turned out to be a mistake. Because I'd been athletic as a young adult, and I still played a mean game of kickball and Ping-Pong, I figured, why not? I lasted three practices.

Concerned that I had failed even in the pursuit of diversion, I was quick to respond when I found a casting call for the annual Irish Play. I did a happy dance when I managed to obtain a one-line part.

Mother, always quick with a word of encouragement, congratulated me immediately. "Even Helen Hayes had to start somewhere," she said, beaming from ear to ear.

Since I learned my line within five minutes, I also signed up to handle the publicity. My first interview was with Steve, the short, lanky gentleman who had snagged the lead. Steve stretched out on the carpet and looked up at me. "So what do you want to know? I'm single, and I haven't had a date in a year and a half."

"Not the sort of interview I had intended," I replied, a bit unnerved by his bold flirting.

It would have ended there, except that when I interviewed the director and the producer they had both sung Steve's praises.

Our first date was the cast party. I wasn't used to dating nice guys—only *pretend* nice guys, who used children and pets to steal a girl's heart. I didn't trust "nice" guys. After all, I had married one and he had deserted me.

Naturally, I was concerned that the budding relationship I had with Steve wouldn't last. Nevertheless, I agreed to a second date, and then a third, and a fourth. Who could say no to a Boy Scout leader? Our next date was a to Boy Scout banquet. It seemed silly to be excited over attending such an event, but Steve was to be the recipient of a prestigious award. He'd asked me to sew a new patch on his Scout uniform for him, and didn't even complain that I had stitched the pocket shut in the process—the first clue that I indeed fit the stereotype of a "dumb" blonde.

I'd hired a sitter who would arrive at 6:00 P.M. and feed the children their dinner so I could at least comb my hair in peace. But, at 6:45 P.M., the sitter had not yet arrived. I called the teenager's home only to discover she had forgotten to let me know she was grounded.

As I hung up the phone, Steve arrived in his highly decorated uniform, looking like a Norman Rockwell painting of the Last American Boy Scout. What would I tell him?

I took out a box of spaghetti and placed a pot of water on the stove while I gave him the bad news.

"Look, why don't you go on ahead," I said. "I'll feed the kids and then try to find another babysitter.

I'll join up with you later." This was a very important moment for him, and I had ruined it.

While three preschool children clung to his neatly pressed khakis, he gave me the only order he has ever spouted in our nearly three decades together: "You get on the phone and find a sitter. I'll make the spaghetti."

Any other man would have run like Peter Rabbit out of Mr. McGregor's garden. Instead, Steve chose to stay through the worst of the crying, spilling, and saucy mess.

I fell in love that night with a man who loved me as I was—a woman who wanted to be accepted for who she was. No pretensions; simply a blonde and a Boy Scout.

Linda Rondeau

Tying the Knot

In the early 1950s, when I was young, I noticed a photograph of a handsome young man on my mother's dresser. I stared at that photograph and imagined that when I was older the handsome young man in the photograph—surely he was Prince Charming—would arrive at my doorstep and sweep me off my feet. We would gallop into the sunset together on his gallant white steed and live happily ever after. Then Mother told me the man in the photograph was my father.

With wide eyes I exclaimed, "That's Daddy?!"

My father didn't look anything like the young man in the photograph. Dad had short wavy, gray hair, not thick brown hair. He looked like a dad, not Prince Charming.

I immediately sat down at the dining room table and asked, "How did you meet Daddy?"

Mother continued ironing Father's shirts as she explained that it all happened when they were in high school.

"I noticed your father in homeroom," she said. "Because I wasn't the prettiest girl in the class, I didn't think he'd pay any attention to me. In study hall, your father sat near me and I wanted to get his attention." She stopped and looked at me, as if hesitant to continue.

"What did you do, Mommy?" I persisted.

"Well, all through study hall, every time I looked at your father, he was studying and not paying any attention to me. So, just before the bell rang, I tied your father's shoelaces to the chair leg," she said in a rush.

I gasped and clapped my hand over my mouth in surprise.

Mama smiled weakly. "When the bell rang, your father jumped up out of his chair and tripped. His face turned beet red and he scrambled to untie the laces before anyone saw. Trying to stifle a giggle I asked, 'Would you like some help, Roy?'"

"You didn't!" I exclaimed.

Mama shrugged. "Well, at least I got your father's attention."

"What happened after that?"

"Well, your father was such a gentleman that he forgave me and began carrying my schoolbooks and walking me to class. Your father was so shy! I began to wonder if he'd ever ask me out on a date. After walking me to class for two months, I invited him to Thanksgiving."

She flipped the shirt and sprayed starch on the collar, and then applied the hot iron once again. Her eyes twinkled as she looked up quickly and tweaked my nose. "I was so excited. When he arrived, I noticed he was wearing his best clothes. Your grandmother was impressed with his kindness and his manners. This was the first time he met your grandparents—he was nervous."

I frowned. "Daddy was nervous? He's not like that now."

Mother flipped the shirt again and ran the iron in and out between the buttons as she continued with her story. "A week later he invited me to go to the movies and your grandparents agreed to let me go on dates with him. We began seeing each other more often and then he asked me to go steady.

"After he gave me his class ring, we started holding hands. I knew then that I had fallen deeply in love with your father. You know it's true love when you hold hands and you can't tell where your hand ends and his hand begins," she explained.

I nodded, eagerly packing away every detail for later retrieval.

"After high school, your father proposed to me. He left town because he had gotten a job in

Connecticut building engines for airplanes. He didn't own a car, but he always found a way to come see me—every weekend—traveling all the way back to Massachusetts. We were engaged for two years.

"I lived at home and took classes to become a nurse. At night, I whiled away the hours embroidering a tablecloth for my trousseau and thinking about our wedding day." She looked at me with a faraway glint in her eyes. "Your father is the only man I have ever loved."

That night at the dinner table, I noticed the way my father looked at my mother, and I recognized that handsome young man from the photo. I sighed happily. It was obvious he was still in love with the woman of his dreams, too.

Laurie M. Doran

Will You?

"Here she comes, Eddie!" I heard one of the telephone company's construction crew members shout half a block ahead of me.

It was a June afternoon in 1950, and I was walking home from my summer job at the Chocolate Shop, a little drugstore in the rural town of Hereford, Texas. I had worked in the drugstore off and on throughout high school. Having just graduated, I planned to register in the fall at West Texas State College in Canyon, which was only thirty miles away.

As another of the workers yelled, I squinted up at the men suspended high on the telephone poles. "You were right, Eddie," he hollered. "She's as cute as a button!" It was then that I realized they were, in fact, talking about me, and a blush slowly spread across my face.

"Hey, Eddie, now's your chance. Ask her," said another man.

Oh, I wanted to turn and run. I can take teasing as well as anyone, but it took sheer willpower to keep moving forward toward those grinning faces.

Suddenly I noticed a man strapped in a cable trolley swing-seat being pulled across the telephone cable line. I recognized him as the boy who had been coming into the Chocolate Shop and ordering one Coke after another, sipping them slowly as he pretended to be looking at a magazine.

"How are you doing?" was his usual question when he sat down on the round swivel stool at the soda fountain.

"Just fine," I would answer, ducking my head in a flirty smile.

He had a carefully combed mass of brown hair. His eyebrows looked bleached on his darkly tanned face. He had a small, slightly crooked nose, full lips, and eyes that matched his blue shirt, exactly.

As I drew closer, the comments flew back and forth, and both Eddie and I felt the effects.

"Here she is, Eddie."

"Are you going to ask her?"

"Don't chicken out."

Eddie was being pulled across the intersection from one telephone pole to another with ropes attached to the cable swing-seat. He shot murderous looks at the crew from a face that had flushed scarlet. Then the rope handlers began to bounce him up and down on the cable, shouting, "Ask her, Eddie. You've got to do it. We aren't going to let you down until you ask her."

I felt a giggle rise up in my throat as I watched the bobbing body above me.

"Come on, guys," Eddie said seriously. "Quit!"

"Not until you ask her. We're going to bounce you until you do it," one man said as they popped the swing-seat up and down, high above the street.

Eddie looked at me and muttered, "Will you go out with me?"

The men hooted and cheered. "Louder! She can't hear you, Eddie."

"Will you go out with me?" Eddie bellowed.

"Yes," I said, watching him dangle in the azure sky.

Strange. My feet suddenly felt cemented to the old brick street, yet my pulse throbbed forcefully in my temples and my heart pounded out a wild cadence in my chest.

We had fun dates all that summer, Eddie and I. In September I left for college, which just happened to be in Eddie's hometown. After my fall semester at West Texas State, Eddie moved back home and enrolled in college so we could be close. We both had full course schedules and jobs, but we saw each other every day.

On April 4, 1951, Eddie and his mother invited two of her women friends and me over for supper. I had eaten there many times and since our first meeting, his mother and I had liked each other. When the dishes were done, his mother announced that she and her friends were going to the store. She winked at Eddie, and then looked at me. "You and Eddie probably have some studying to do."

I put my books on the dining room table and opened my notebook. Eddie set his books on the table, too, but did not open them. I heard his mother's 1948 Ford back out of the driveway and watched as Eddie got a glass of water, tore some pages from his notepad, examined his pencil lead, and stared at his books. Then he let his dog in, rubbed the dog's head, and cupped the dog's face in his hands.

"Are you hungry?" he asked me, without looking up.

I shook my head. "We just ate."

"Would you like something to drink? I could make some coffee."

I shrugged. "Okay, if you want some."

Just then a car pulled into the driveway. Eddie quickly stepped out on the front porch and waved the car away. I thought I heard him say, "Not yet." Puzzled by his behavior, I glanced up at him as he came back to the table. "It's hot in here," he said. "Are you hot?"

"No."

"Would you like some iced tea?"

"No, thank you," I said as I closed my book.

Suddenly, he reached for my hand. "I have something for you," he said. His hand felt cold as he led me to the front bedroom and took a little black velvet box out of the dresser. He snapped the box open and lifted up a diamond ring between his thumb and forefinger.

At that instant, his mother and her two friends burst into the house. "Did you ask her?"

Flustered, Eddie nearly shouted, "You didn't stay gone long enough to give me a chance!"

His mother threw her arms up in despair. "We drove around and around the block several times. How long does it take for you to ask her?"

Eddie looked at his mother the same way he had looked at the phone crew. Undaunted by the glare on Eddie's face, his mother and her friends crowded around us anxiously. "Well?" one friend asked.

Eddie turned to me, sucked in his breath like he was going to dive underwater, and asked, "Will you accept this engagement ring?"

"Yes," I whispered.

Strange: The same feelings that had swept over me the day I stood beneath the cable swing-seat rushed over me again. My feet felt glued to the old wooden floor, but my pulse throbbed in my temples

with renewed vigor, and my heart pounded errati-
cally in my chest.

Today, these cherished memories are sweet to
recall. Eddie and I have shrouded them in laughter
and held them close to our hearts for fifty-three years
and counting.

Emmarie Lehnick

Family Traditions

For my family, Fourth of July celebrations have always followed a long-established pattern. In the morning, we joined crowds of familiar faces gathered along tree-lined streets to watch the parade. Little League district champions waved from the back of a borrowed flatbed, bright sunlight bouncing off brilliant white uniforms. Boy Scouts and a band or two marched by. With their red fezzes wobbling precariously atop snowy hair, laughing Shriners cut figure-eights on tiny scooters. The parade never lasted long, and afterward, we hurried to backyard barbeques or potluck block parties where the men played horseshoes and the kids ran three-legged races. When the sunlight faded, the party moved to the high school football stadium. There we endured the speeches, knowing it would soon be time to rush the field—for everyone had a favorite spot where they always spread their blanket. Atop blankets to protect our sun-warmed skin from the scratchy grass, we exclaimed over brilliant fireworks bursting against a cloudless sky.

All of that changed on the Fourth of July when my father-in-law died.

Although ten years have passed since he died, I still don't know why Dad's death came as such a shock. The whole family had seen his wiry strength fade, heard the deepening of his raspy voice, witnessed the coughing fits that wracked his body and left him gasping for breath. We told ourselves that if it were something serious, he would be under a doctor's care. It was, but he wasn't. He insisted he was fine, and we all played the game. Even in his final hours, my mother-in-law maintained the charade, doling out aspirin and agreeing not to call an ambulance, until his chest pains became too intense to ignore. At the hospital, not even the reality of death could penetrate the layers of her denial. She insisted there was no one—really, no one—to call, until a nurse more determined than she finally pried a name from the tightly clenched mind and sent a ball of grief rolling our way.

Game over.

I suspect the news hit my daughter harder than the rest of us. She was home alone that Fourth of July. When the telephone rang in the middle of the night, she was barely nineteen and far too young to field calls bearing such tragic news. Far too young to find her way down unfamiliar roads to a strange hospital, yet she did. She handled everything with remarkable strength, even managing to take her grandmother home to an empty house and to spend the next few hours burying her own grief while she gave comfort and made phone calls, until the word spread and the rest of the family tore across the state to their side.

For the next ten years, Independence Day was known as "the day Dad died." The entire family side-stepped national traditions of cookouts and fireworks while new customs, notably less festive ones, took their place. July 4 became a day to visit and console my mother-in-law, the day we unsuccessfully tried to assuage our collective guilt at not realizing the truth.

Telephones that ring in the middle of the night rarely bring good news. So I feared the worst when ours rang late at night on another Fourth of July. This time, through the magic of wireless electronics, I heard my daughter. She was giggling, laughing, ecstatically happy. The man she loves had proposed and, at her speechless nod, slipped a ring with a diamond the size of Mt. Rushmore on her finger. She was delirious, oblivious to the clock on the wall. This news could not wait until morning.

On opposite ends of the telephone line, champagne corks popped and celebrations—Fourth of July celebrations—ensued. The couple had been dating for a year, so their engagement wasn't nearly as much of a surprise as was its timing. My daughter's fiancé—a new word in my lexicon—did not understand the significance of his chosen date. A good, kind man, he had grown up in America's Heartland and had no reason to think of Independence Day as anything but a happy occasion. And for that I am grateful. If he had known our family history, he might have delayed his proposal, and what a shame that would have been.

As congratulations flowed and best wishes were exchanged, I once more sensed old traditions slipping away as new ones moved in to take their place. By the time we had said our goodbyes and hung up our phones, the day Dad died had undergone another metamorphosis. In the future, it will be known as the day our daughter became engaged. For the happy couple, and the family they will make, the Fourth of July will once more become a time of celebration, of backyard picnics and fireworks—lots of fireworks.

My daughter deserves that. Somehow, I think Dad would approve.

Lee Rhuday

On Rodent Feet

Too often, I find myself longing for the splashy show of romance, featuring diamonds and limousines. Never mind that I told my husband I didn't like diamonds because they were cold stones or that I've never been in a limousine—ever. In fact, I would be astounded to even see a limousine in our tiny rural town. But every now and again, I think along those lines. I guess it's all of the Christmas commercials featuring well-groomed couples holding hands and staring lovingly at one another. If that's not enough, there's always the voice-over explaining that love is expressed with a four-carat stone that suddenly looks anything but cold.

For a moment, I am tempted. Then, clear as a bell, the voices of my children arguing in the next room remind me that maybe our family isn't exactly the diamonds and limousine type. Besides, when it comes to Christmas, my husband expects me to pick out my own gift.

I remember those early years when he tried to shop for me. The ugliest dress known to mankind appeared under our Christmas tree with my name attached. It was a hideous combination of a flag for some newly formed country and a military uniform, complete with epaulets and brass buttons. Who was this man who thought I'd actually like it? Had he never paid attention to the clothes I wore? I swallowed with difficulty, smiled, and thanked him. The real problem came later when I tried to fish out the name of the store so I could exchange it.

Every year since, my husband asks for the exact store name, model number, and color of the desired gift so we won't have the dress episode again. While it's thoughtful that he wants to get the perfect gift, somehow it's disappointing that he doesn't know me well enough to know what the gift should be. Just another twist on the "if you loved me, I wouldn't have to tell you" theme. Besides, we're both over forty; big romantic gestures are long behind us.

As always, on this particular year, Christmas came and went quickly. I was very pleased with the camera I had picked out for myself and my husband was equally pleased with his gift certificate to the local sports store. Then things turned bad. An unannounced heavy snowfall trapped us in the house together for a few days with nothing to do except sit in front of the fire and watch TV. My husband, of course, watched sports and assorted odd talk shows, leaving me to watch the antics of Chunky, our family guinea pig.

Chunky, the class pet for several of my special education classes, had been forced to retire because one of the custodians considered him a rat and refused to clean my classroom. As guinea pigs go, Chunky was generally a happy fellow. Every morning, he greeted me with a squeal—his way of begging for a baby carrot or a lettuce leaf. But as the snow fell and I continued to watch Chunky, I realized he wasn't as lively as usual. Somewhat subdued, my last thought before climbing into bed that night was that age catches up to all of us, even guinea pigs.

The next morning Chunky was lying on his side breathing hard. No amount of celery or apple tidbits could get him back on his feet. My husband started calling vets everywhere, and eventually found one that was still open. According to the vet, Chunky had experienced a stroke and the only decent thing left to do was to put him to sleep. I signed the paperwork and turned away so no one would see my tears fall.

We drove quite a while before I said anything. It was too hard to talk. Chunky had been a member of our family for years. Once we got home, my son moved Chunky's cage out to the garage so I didn't have to see it. I know he meant well, but that seemed to make matters worse.

Then my husband gathered up the children to go rent some videos. I frowned. Sarah and Josh couldn't agree on anything, and he knew it. Then I realized my husband was giving me a moment of solitude—he was doing what he could to give me space. Instead of questioning his motives, I let them go without a word.

When I heard the car doors slam again some time later, I waited for the inevitable whine about who didn't get what they wanted. Instead, my daughter skipped into the room with a smile. My husband followed with a small box in his hands. He placed it gently in my lap and then left the room. The scratching confirmed my suspicions long before the tiny black-and-white face peered out at me.

"He saw you cry so he bought you a guinea pig," my daughter explained.

I was dumbfounded. But as the little guinea pig continued to scratch, I had to admit that it was just possible that my husband and I weren't too old for grand romantic gestures, after all. In that moment, I learned that love comes in all shapes and forms. Sometimes it even comes on tiny little rodent feet.

Carole Wyatt

When It Began

The afternoon sun filtered through a maple tree and cast leafy shadows across the floor of the porch and over the tea table. My mother Rita sat on the wicker loveseat, her four-pound poodle on her lap. I sat in an Adirondack chair next to them, my pencil poised above a notepad.

I knew the family anecdote: Dad had pushed Mom down the stairs when he was three years old and she was two. She hit her cheek on a shoe scraper and it left a scar. Having scarred her, he had to marry her. The old stories were told piecemeal, amid laughter, but what I wanted now was a picture of the real love story in sequence—especially because Dad, at the age of eighty-seven and after sixty-four years of marriage, had passed away.

"Mom, I know that you and Dad grew up next door to each other and that you eloped, but tell me the details. When did Dad tell you he loved you?"

Mother pursed her lips and looked at the porch ceiling. "I'm not sure he did. I really don't remember. I think he just hinted at it."

"Well, then, how did he ask you to marry him? Didn't he get down on his knees or something?"

Mother scratched her poodle's ears. "I don't think he ever asked me to marry him. I think he just told me we were going to get married."

"If he didn't tell you he loved you or ask you to marry him, how did it all come about? How did you know you loved each other? Was it while you were dating?"

Mom set her poodle on the cushion beside her and picked up a shortbread cookie from the tea table. "We never actually dated."

I was afraid that getting the real story would not be easy. I began to doodle on my notepad, hoping that I was not asking too much of her since Dad had died only one year earlier.

"Did you just decide you loved him enough to marry him that day, when he asked you—I mean, told you?" I looked at her skeptically. "When did your love for each other begin?"

Mom poured herself a cup of tea, and stirred in sugar and cream. She knitted her brows, concentrating as she remembered her youth in Fort Scott, Kansas. "I think I always knew I loved him."

A warm breeze ruffled through the herb garden and blew a scent of rosemary across the porch. Mother sipped her tea delicately and then smiled.

"Even as a little kid, Ken was thoughtful. He always opened doors for his mother and grandma and helped them into the house with groceries. He was a football player and wrestler, yet he was musically talented. He played the guitar and sang songs he had written. We both played cello in the junior high school orchestra— I sat first chair and he sat in the back. When I was just a little girl, Ken's grandma told me, 'Honey, you go after Kenny. He's the best of the bunch.'

"The closest thing to a date we ever had was when I was sixteen. I hosted a dance at my grand-mother's house and invited the Thompson boys. Ken came with his little brother, Gerald. They sat in the window seat the entire evening—never danced once. But after everyone else had left, Ken came back, driving his parents' Buick, and took me for a spin, with Gerald in the rumble seat.

"During the Depression, Ken's family rented their home and moved away from Fort Scott, trying to make a living in the insurance business. By the time they returned, I was in college at Kansas University. Whenever I would come home on weekends, Ken would come over to visit with me. We often sat on the steps of the front porch and talked. We were good friends . . . buddies.

"It was on Saturday, March 11, 1939, just before I graduated with a degree in cello, that Ken told me we were going to get married. Right then, that day. We decided to keep it a secret. Ken's cousin, Jack McQuitty, and his wife, Lavonne, drove us to the county seat in Girard. After we got our license, we looked in the phonebook, found the number for the First Christian Church, and got in touch with the minister. Since it was evening by that time, we were married in the home of Reverend Northcott. Jack and Lavonne and the minister's wife were witnesses. The Northcott's little boy ambled down the stairs in his pajamas and yawned throughout the wedding ceremony."

From where we sat, we watched as a scarlet cardinal and his mate, feathered in soft olive-browns with red undertones, landed in the bird feeder. The male picked up a sunflower seed and fed it to his mate.

Mother smiled. "Ain't love grand?"

I nodded. "Yes, it is." I wondered at her peaceful acceptance of whatever life brings—even its closure. Then it dawned on me—she still talks about Dad in the present tense.

I glanced at her and caught a faraway look in her eyes. "Mom, tell me some more details. Did you have music? Did you carry something old, something new, something borrowed, something blue?"

Mom settled more comfortably into her chair and grinned. "Well, we didn't have any music. Nothing new. But our clothes were old." We both cackled, startling the cardinals.

Mom's face glowed as she remembered. "We borrowed Lavonne's wedding ring, and I wore a navy blue suit. That's three out of the essential four. Must have brought us good luck, because our marriage certainly lasted.

"After the wedding, we celebrated at a hamburger joint and then went home. We didn't have any money or a place to be alone together. So Ken spent the night in his house and I spent the night in mine. We each woke our parents and told them that we had gotten married. No one seemed surprised."

Satisfied that she had, at last, spit out the bare bones of the story, Mom poured herself another cup of tea while her poodle crawled from her lap onto her ample bosom and snuggled beneath her chin. I looked at my mother's serene face and realized that she had never been without my father—ever. Their love affair had begun when he was three years old and she was two, and he is with her still.

Nancy Gustafson

Could Love Get Any Sweeter?

I honestly didn't think love could get sweeter than the day I walked down the aisle in June of 1983. There he stood, my friend and love, and his smile was just for me. He was tall, handsome, and blue-eyed, and I found it hard to believe that I, a farm girl from Charlo, Montana—population 212—could have ever ended up with such a special guy.

There were bumps along the way, yes. Angry words? Some. But that first year passed like a golden dream. We were young and in love, and everything was new and precious.

Then came the morning we gave birth to our first child. Could anything be dearer than my husband's eyes holding mine during each intense contraction? Unless, perhaps, it would be the picture of him cradling our tiny daughter in suddenly large hands. Our world had expanded beyond the two of us, yet somehow our love was not diluted, it was strengthened.

When baby two and baby three came along, each advent was deeply precious. Could anything be sweeter than watching him romp with the children, chase them around the house, or carry them horse-back to bed? Our eyes often met over little blond heads, and his smile was the same one I saw on the day he waited for me to walk down the aisle. No, not exactly the same, it was an older smile. More knowing, yet still choosing to gaze deeply into mine. I have to say, it was, if anything, sweeter than it had been seven years before—distilled from all of our shared trials and triumphs—and stronger for the struggles.

More years passed, bringing added challenges—a move to the Midwest, three more dear babies, church upheavals, career changes. We were like birds, flying from nest to food and back to nest, nonstop. These were the dangerous years—so easy to lose contact with one another and slip into coexistence due to the sheer effort that it took to parent, supply, and run such a household. Questions surfaced: "Who am I, really? What happened to all of my dreams, my inten-tion to accomplish great things on this earth?" Amid diapers and dinners and piles of laundry, I wondered if I was even the same girl who had floated up that aisle with aspirations as wide as the world itself.

Had my friend and love changed as well?

He's still tall, still handsome, now with a distinguishing shade of gray frosting his temples. But each morning as I search the blue of his eyes, I find the same man looking back at me. It is the old, familiar gaze, yet somehow deeper, more intensely purposeful. And in his eyes I read encouragement and support.

"Be a writer," he says. "You have things to say. You're still the person you were when I first met you."

Strangely, I realize he is right. Perhaps he's seeing the same thing happening in my eyes as I see in his. I'm not sure. But I do know one thing: We're twenty-two years into our honeymoon journey, and every morning he still wakes me up with a cup of coffee and a kiss, and I still think, Could love get any sweeter?

Leslie J. Wyatt

A Dream Wedding

"Beautiful, spirited, and fun to be with" describes my cousin Jeannie, who will celebrate her forty-fifth wedding anniversary this year. Gloria Jean Collum Dunsford is my closest cousin. I was the maid of honor at her wedding, and this is her remarkable story.

When Jeannie was two years old she was diagnosed with muscular dystrophy. My aunt and uncle were told that she would not live to the age of twenty, and recommended that she be institutionalized before the family became too attached to her. Aunt Eileen, a strong-minded individual of Nova Scotia stock, would not accept such a decree. She was determined to have her daughter participate as fully as possible in life. Long before mainstreaming children with special needs was a priority in schools, Aunt Eileen made sure Jeannie was, in fact, mainstreamed.

Each day she pulled Jeannie to school in a little red wagon so she could be with children her own age, doing what everyone else was doing.

When Jeannie was ten years old, the small town of Avon, Massachusetts, held a collection and bought a wheelchair for Jeannie, and all of the children competed to be the one to push her around. In high school, before ramps were mandatory in all town buildings, the boys actually lined up to lift her wheel-chair up the steps of the school entrance.

In the 1950s, Avon didn't offer much in the area of recreation for teenagers. So, for fun and entertain-ment, I would push Jeannie to "the square," which consisted of a couple of churches, a drugstore, a fire station, a post office, a variety store, and a place to have a hamburger and listen to Elvis on the jukebox. Since Jeannie couldn't go in, I'd bring out vanilla Cokes and we'd hang out with friends, listening to Elvis sing his heart out through the screen door.

During the summer, Jeannie's family and another family spent their vacation camping at Nickerson State Park on Cape Cod. Each summer, I also vis-ited with Jeannie for a couple of weeks. By the time we were teenagers, a daily routine of swimming and going out in the rowboat had been established. Aunt Eileen pushed the wheelchair to the edge of the hill, carried Jeannie down to the beach, and lifted her either into the water or into the boat. Once Jeannie was in the boat, I would row us across Flax Pond. Despite having lost significant muscular strength by this time, Jeannie could still balance herself in the boat.

In February of 1957, Jeannie and I went on a double date to a "Sock Hop" at the American Legion Hall. It was Charlie and Jeannie's first date. He was twenty and about to enter the army, and she was seventeen. The date had been arranged by a mutual friend, from Cape Cod, which was also Charlie's hometown. They enjoyed each other's company so well that they began to correspond as soon as Charlie entered the service.

Two years later, Charlie's proposal came by mail, all the way from Germany, where he was stationed at the time. Initially, Jeannie rejected his proposal. Her mother had always been her primary caretaker and she wasn't sure Charlie understood what would be required of him. But Charlie, also of Nova Scotia stock, wouldn't take no for an answer. Eventually, he convinced Jeannie and her family that he had read everything about muscular dystrophy and knew exactly what he was doing, and that he loved Jeannie very much. Finally, with fingers crossed, Jeannie accepted his proposal.

Coincidentally, at that same time WMEX, a popular radio station, was holding a Dream Wedding Contest. Jeannie, then twenty, entered the contest and won. The prize included the flowers, her gown, photographs, and a reception for 100 people. It was an unbelievable gift. No one in the family had enough money to pay for such an elaborate wedding!

That wonderful day will live on in my mind forever. There wasn't a dry eye in the Avon Baptist Church. After the ceremony, Charlie carried Jeannie from the door of the church all the way down the walkway to the car. There, on the sprawling green lawn outside the church, the whole town waited to congratulate the new couple! But my clearest memory of that day was during the reception, when Charlie lifted Jeannie out of the wheelchair to swirl her around the room, carrying her in his arms for their first dance as husband and wife.

Not much later, I stood beside my dear, anxious aunt when Charlie carried his bride out the door on the way to their honeymoon. I was also present the next week when they returned from Cape Cod. Charlie strode through the door with the love of his life in his arms. Laughing, he gently tossed Jeannie onto the couch in a happy heap. She was sporting a new haircut—fashioned by his own hand—which was easier for him to handle. Then, with a sly smile, he complained that the seamed nylon stockings women wore were a stupid invention.

"You just can't get them on straight!" he said, grinning from ear to ear.

Forty-five years later, the happy couple is still in love and enjoying each day together. Jeannie's muscular capacity has diminished considerably over the years, and she's had some very close calls. Following recent major surgery she wrote me and said: "I'm in Charlie's good hands and he has pulled me through another crisis with his strength and abiding love—along with my tenacious grip on life."

As I read that passage I was reminded of the day Charlie swept Jeannie up in his very capable arms and whisked her out through the church door, eager to start their new life together, and I thought again: Jeannie is right—she is in good hands.

Linda M. Wolk

Two-Dollar Wife

"That's the best two dollars I ever spent—marrying that old secondhand woman," Uncle Bill exclaimed. "She's the best thing that ever happened to me. I'd never tell her that, though, and don't you tell her either, young'un."

It was a warm spring afternoon and I couldn't think of a better place to spend my time than with Uncle Bill on the porch of his small home in Dublin, Texas. Side by side we inhaled an enticing smell—unique to his home at this time of the year—a combination of car exhaust and antique roses.

Uncle Bill spent much of his time right here in this same spot, watching the cars go by on Highway 67, thinking of all the places he had been and all the people he had known and loved. In his eighty-five years, he'd traveled from the family farm in Comanche, Texas, to the battlefields of France and

Germany, to postwar Japan, finally returning to Texas to live out his days. For more than fifty of those years, Aunt Loez had been by his side. Theirs is a love story that had always inspired me. In a world where everything—including marriage—was disposable, this lifelong partnership of two humble people was a testament to love and the human spirit.

I knew this might be our last visit together, and I wanted to hear all the stories and say all the things that needed to be said. So, naturally, I asked him to tell me one more time about how Aunt Loez became his Two-Dollar Wife.

He sat awhile, his mischievous green eyes taking on a faraway look from beneath thick bushy eyebrows, and his strong, thrusting jaw unmoving. Today, he was dressed in red sweats and a blue baseball cap that read: OLD FART. A fancy black and white checked apron—handmade by Aunt Loez—covered a catheter bag and helped to disguise the fact that his war-damaged kidneys had almost ceased to function.

In the house, I heard the scurrying feet of my aunt as she tended to something or another. Uncle Bill heard her, too. He nodded his head in the direction of the front door.

"That woman takes care of everything," he said proudly. "Whatever needs to be done, she can do it. She can handle those bills—the medical forms—all those things. I don't know what I'd do without her.

But there were some problems to begin with, and it almost didn't happen."

Uncle Bill and Aunt Loez were children of the Depression, both from large farm families in central Texas. At the age of sixteen, Bill left home for the Civilian Conservation Corps, then the Army. Loez left for a marriage that ended badly, leaving her with emotional scars and a small son to support. Needing to put food on the table for herself and her son, she moved to San Antonio where she obtained work as a military driver, doing her part for the war effort while at the same time supporting her family.

Although they came from the same area, their paths didn't cross until 1943 when Bill's sister Velma, who was married to Loez's brother Hulbert, decided that their siblings were meant for each other and promptly set about matchmaking. The two were not immediately impressed with each other, however. Loez was still wary of men in general and Bill was concerned about her divorcee status, which was uncommon at the time. She was, in his elegant phrasing, a "secondhand woman." Still, they were drawn to each other, and love did eventually conquer all—according to Uncle Bill their love was worth the $2 he paid for the marriage license.

On a sunny day in June 1944, home on leave and waiting to be shipped overseas, Bill was painting his parents' house in Dublin when he suddenly put the brush down, walked into town, and hopped on the next bus for San Antonio. He walked in the pouring rain from the bus stop to Loez's boarding house and asked her to marry him. Decisions had to be made quickly in the war years. Loez said yes and climbed aboard the bus back to Dublin with him. They were married a few days later in his sister's house in Comanche.

As I think about the love shared between these two unlikely people, a smile comes to my face. Although their financial status is evident, their personalities are what you recognize when you enter their modest home. The walls are covered with hand-lettered signs such as: "FROWNING IS AGAINST THE LAW IN HERE" and "NO COMPLAINING ZONE." Poems and letters from grandchildren are interspersed among dozens of family photos. It is a home lacking in material goods, but rich beyond measure in things that can't be bought.

Comfortable with one another, we sat quietly, watching the cars whiz by. Gently, the chilly blanket of twilight fell around us, and before we knew it, Aunt Loez was at the door telling Uncle Bill that it was time to come inside.

Uncle Bill grumbled. "We better get inside before that old woman blows a gasket. But you know, that was the best two dollars I ever spent, marrying that secondhand woman. Don't you tell her I said that."

I patted his knee and turned the wheelchair toward the door. "I'll never tell," I said as a rectangle of warm yellow light spilled out the open door, and Uncle Bill went back inside to his Two-Dollar Wife.

Shirley H. Wetzel

Daddy's Little Girl

My daughter said she wanted the simplest of weddings. She wanted to wear white, walk down the aisle of our church, kiss her Daddy goodbye at the altar, and marry the man of her dreams in front of a hometown crowd of family and friends. For her reception she wanted a party where everyone could kick back and have a good time.

"Rent a tent. Get a couple of kegs, order in an old-time Southern feast of baked beans and finger-lickin' good barbecue." That's what she said throughout high school, and college, and even later, after she joined the Navy.

I suspected things might change someday, and I was right. Once the third finger of her left hand bent under the weight of a flawless one-carat diamond, mundane conversations about work and car repairs gave way to discussions of the advantages of silk over tulle, dried flowers over fresh, and where to find a hall large enough—and elegant enough—to accommodate all her friends. The engaged couple planned to marry far from our Florida home and, as my hopes for Meemaw's Barbeque faded, money woes surfaced.

"We put her through college. She's been on her own for five years. Why do we have to pay anything for the wedding?" my husband asked.

I swallowed the words, "Silly boy," and instead replied, "Since they both have good jobs, Emily Post says we don't have to pay for the wedding. But we should pitch in. Agreed?"

My husband gave me a wary look. "How much?"

"Three thousand would pay for a nice wedding here, but not in a big city in Maryland. We could give them that much. They'll have to pay the rest themselves."

"The rest?" he winced. "It's only one day! How much more could it cost?"

I could hardly fault him for asking. Like most girls in our small town, I had walked down the aisle in a $100, off-the-rack dress with only my sister as an attendant. We had a cake and fruit punch reception in the church fellowship hall. A mere twenty-eight years later, our daughter argued the merits of a five-hour open bar and explained her pressing need for six bridesmaids.

We needed a battle plan. We flew to Maryland, gushed over the ring, and settled in for a serious talk. Surrounded by bridal magazines, catering menus, and price sheets, the bride-to-be had plans of her own. Billboard-size dollar signs flashed red neon before my eyes as she described the new-and-improved wedding of her dreams.

I shouldered the dirty work. "Daddy and I want you to have the best, honey, but we don't have that kind of money."

Beautiful blue eyes welled with tears. I gulped and looked to my husband. Emotions I'd never seen before colored his face.

With sad, puppy dog eyes, he sought his little girl's approval. "Sweetheart, your mother and I want to pay half. How much will that be?"

"I don't know, Daddy," she murmured. "We don't have a final cost yet."

The strange emotions I had just seen faded from my husband's face as he once more became the practical engineer I knew and loved. "Let's get on the computer and work it up," he said with a grin.

Two hours later they were the proud owners of a working budget whose bottom line could put food on the table of every man, woman, and child in our hometown for a month. That night, as we climbed into bed, my husband turned to me.

"It isn't enough," he sighed.

I had to ask. "What isn't enough?"

"She's my only little girl. We should pay for the whole wedding."

I flipped the lights back on and stared into the familiar features of a man I did not recognize. "You didn't want to pay for any of it. And then you offered half."

"It doesn't feel right. We should pay it all," he repeated.

This unexpected side of my husband flabbergasted me into silence. The man I married wears the same sports coat for five years, the same suit for ten. He believes that things with electrical plugs make excellent Christmas gifts. He refers to our ten-year-old Buick as "the new car" and refuses to consider a trade-in until the odometer trips over . . . twice.

"Who are you, and what have you done with my husband?" I asked the new man in my bed. I wasn't sure I wanted the old one back. This new guy had possibilities.

I reached for the acid test. "We'd have to take out a loan." The new guy didn't flinch.

"Okay," he said. "We'll do it."

With no further discussion, he rolled over and fell asleep. I rolled over, too, but it was a long time before I slept.

Our daughter's wedding took a year to plan, and the new guy enjoyed every minute of it. Still masquerading as my husband, he walked his designer-clad little girl down a rose-strewn aisle, kissed her sweetly on the cheek, and handed her off to her soon-to-be husband. Afterward, we had the party of all parties, perfect down to the last exquisitely expensive detail. Sipping champagne and listening to the music, I teased my husband.

"So, how about a trip to Hawaii for the mother and father of the bride?"

"Hawaii," he snorted. "We can't afford Hawaii."

I searched everywhere, but the new guy had done his job and was nowhere to be found. Just wait, I tell myself. We have a son and someday he'll get married. That new guy will reappear. When he does, I'll buy tickets to Honolulu before the first boutonniere gets ordered. But my heart knows better. Things will be different when our son gets married.

When that day comes, another man will walk the bride down the aisle. Another man will blink back tears as he gives the bride away. And, despite the empty pockets of his rented tuxedo, another father will insist on the perfect wedding for "Daddy's little girl."

Lee Rhuday

Someone Old,
Someone New

Nestled among the maple trees in Silver Creek, New York, sits an irresistibly charming retirement home overlooking the shores of Lake Erie. This little English Tudor and sprawling grounds used to be the home of an equally enchanting elderly woman. Her name was Anna, and she was one of my favorite people in the whole world.

For three years, I made the weekly half-hour trip to visit her, first as a volunteer, but soon as a best friend. The two of us loved the beauty of the surrounding woods. Whenever the weather permitted, we would walk leisurely along the pathways and talk about anything and everything.

Anna took a great interest in my life, so when I told her I had fallen in love, she wanted to meet the man I couldn't help but ramble on about. His name was Tom, and he had an incredibly warm and inviting personality, the kind that I knew Anna would love. Without hesitation, Tom enthusiastically agreed to accompany me on one of my visits. The very next week I brought him along, and he instantly adored Anna's light-hearted spirit. From that day forward, Tom, Anna, and I spent many Sunday afternoons meandering through the woods, just sharing stories and laughing the day away.

I loved watching Tom interact with Anna. He was gentle in a way that I had never seen before and was always able to get her to do what seemed like the impossible to others.

"C'mon Annie, the doctors all love you and miss your smiling face," Tom would say with a sparkle in his eye. When he'd hold her hand and tell her everything was okay, I somehow felt as if it were my hand he was holding. My admiration for him grew as the weeks went on, and we were virtually inseparable by the end of that first year.

As Anna neared her ninety-fifth birthday, she needed the help of a wheelchair to get around, and our strolls in the woods eventually had to be replaced by visits to the gazebo. Every Sunday, Anna insisted that we lovebirds run along and have some fun of our own, yet Tom and I were both as passionate about helping her as we were about each other. Her presence only drew us closer to one another, and we would have much rather run errands with her than catch some dinner and a movie.

When Anna's birthday came upon us, I envisioned taking her out to the woods one last time. Tom asserted that it would be much too risky to navigate the wheelchair over the stone-laden pathway, so I reluctantly accepted that we would have to alter our plans. Since Anna loved the outdoors, I packed a picnic lunch and figured we could eat in the courtyard gardens and view the picturesque woods from afar. As the three of us made our way out the back door, Mike, the groundskeeper, came puttering up on his golf cart, waving to Tom. To my amazement, he pulled up alongside us, shut off the engine, and dismounted. He jingled the keys in his hand, and joked, "Your chariot awaits you!"

My heart leapt when I realized that Tom had arranged this and intended to take us out to our most cherished place after all! Excitedly, we drove down the grassy path and into the woods. I was utterly speechless when we arrived at our destination. A table and chairs stood amidst the wooded backdrop, adorned with red foil hearts, along with a dozen roses in a vase. A banner reading "I love you, Sherry" hung from the trees. As I walked toward the wondrous sight, Tom grabbed my hand, knelt down, and asked me to marry him. When he put the ring on my finger, all three of us had tears in our eyes. Then a sly smile swept across Anna's face.

"I kept the cat in the bag!" she remarked proudly.

We spent the entire afternoon there. Together, we celebrated two very special events and created one of the most memorable days of our lives.

Sheryl Puchalski

Asking Dad

I met Laura, the love of my life, at Michigan State University when I was a sophomore and she was a freshman. It wasn't love at first sight or anything magical like that, and I soon found you couldn't ask for two more opposite people.

Laura came from the big city of Detroit, while I grew up in a rural area in mid-Michigan with fewer people than the population of our dorm at MSU. She was the youngest child in a family of four kids and I was the oldest of three kids. Laura came from a devoutly Catholic family, whereas my family rarely attended the Protestant church we claimed as our own. Laura had attended private Catholic schools from kindergarten through high school. It was a bit different from my public school education with much of the learning carried out in a one-room schoolhouse. And while Laura's folks weren't rich, their economic status was considerably above that of my family. I'd grown up hunting and fishing; Laura hated guns, and I don't think she'd ever gone fishing. About the only thing our families had in common was that our parents both lived in red-brick houses. Of course, Laura's family home was a four-bedroom two-story. Ours was a converted one-room schoolhouse, only a couple of miles from the one I had attended.

Despite our differences—and I thank the Lord daily for this—Laura and I came to love one another. Now, I'll be honest and say I don't remember actually asking Laura to marry me all those years ago; we just sort of decided we should get married. But the thing I do remember most clearly was the requirement to ask her father for her hand in marriage. That is an event I remember very well.

While I was positive Laura was the one for me, the idea of asking her father for permission nearly scared me away. From my perspective, I faced an uphill battle with a number of things against me. I'd met her father only a couple of times and he hadn't gotten my name right either time. I come from a family with deep rural roots. My grandfather was a lumberjack and farmer, my grandmother a house-keeper and gardener. My dad drove a truck and my mom worked as a nurse's aide. Laura's dad worked in management and supervision for a drug company, while her mom was a district manager for the Avon

Company. But the two biggest things against me, and what I felt would be the hardest to overcome, were (1) I wasn't Catholic, and (2) I was asking for the hand of their youngest daughter.

In spite of it all, I gathered up my courage and picked a weekend to visit her folks. In the weeks before the trip I carefully planned out my speech, going over it time and time again—day after day—until I felt confident he'd say yes. I was still worried as all get-out, but as we drove south from East Lansing, I was sure I had the right words to convince Laura's dad of my worthiness to be his son-in-law. I just needed to stick to my plan.

My plan called for us to arrive on Saturday, spend a nice afternoon and evening with Laura's folks, and then I would ask her dad if I could have a word with him on Sunday before we headed back to school. Things started going awry the minute we arrived. Instead of a quiet evening with just her folks, Laura's entire family showed up. I quickly learned that when the family gathered they played a game called Michigan Rummy (also known as Tripoly). And they played it for money.

It wasn't much money—just pennies—but I figured if they played for money they must take it seriously. Indeed they did. As we sat down around the big kitchen table, I learned I couldn't sit next to Laura because couples weren't allowed to sit with each other (to avoid cheating). So there I sat, between two people I didn't know, playing a game I'd never played, trying to impress a family I hoped to join. Of course, as the night progressed, I came to know the family, but I also had beginner's luck. When the game ended, I was up by a couple of dollars and smiling big until I learned that Laura's dad—who never lost money at this game—was down by a couple of dollars. I later learned that this was not a big deal to him. But at the time, perhaps due to my somewhat different economic point of view, I figured I'd just made the challenge of asking for Laura's hand more difficult.

Slowly the others made their departures. Finally, it was just Laura's parents and the two of us. Laura's mom went to straighten up the kitchen and Laura headed downstairs to the basement to put in a load of laundry. I started to join her when she reminded me this would be a good time to ask her dad if he and I could speak the next day. So I walked into the front room and took a chair near him as he watched TV. When a commercial came I on, I took a deep breath and asked if he and I could talk the next day. Letting out a sigh of relief, I leaned back, thinking of my speech for the next day. Then he surprised me by saying, "Let's talk now."

My speech disappeared from my head. My palms began sweating. Somehow I managed to tell him I wanted to marry Laura. My plan had called for me to ask him if I could ask her, but now I just wanted to get it out before I lost my nerve. His willingness to talk then hadn't been part of the plan, nor had I expected him to ask questions, which he did. When did we plan to marry? What were my future plans? How was I going to support her? And perhaps the hardest question of all: Where did I stand with the military draft?

I don't recall my exact words, but I gave the answers as best I could. They must've been good enough, because he gave his permission, and then he suggested we get the women, as he put it, and all talk it over.

Obviously, it all worked out. Thirty-eight yeas later, Laura and I have three wonderful children and two perfect grandsons. And just last December, I was in Laura's dad's place when my youngest daughter's beau asked to talk to Laura and me privately. Of course, things have changed and he didn't so much ask for permission as announce he was going to ask her, but I could tell his nerves were strung just as tightly as mine had been all those years ago. So, of course, I said yes.

Bob Davis

Not an Ordinary Patch of Grass

To some, it may have looked like an old, ordinary patch of grass. To me, it defied words. My hill—a gently rising, majestic wonder of my childhood world—tantalized me. Each summer, I tasted nearly every blade of grass as my sister and I rolled and somersaulted down my hill. Our wagons and bikes left their marks in the dewy grass in the warm mornings and evenings, and on some evenings I envisioned my hill as a major city lit by the flickering lights of hundreds of lightning bugs. I saw my hill in many different ways, but never in my wildest dreams would I have envisioned my hill in the splendor that it would one day hold, when I was much older.

My hill was special for many reasons, but it was my dad's touch that would make it extraordinary. Every summer, he mixed a special fertilizer concoction and then walked to the top of my grassy hill and carefully fertilized the letters of both my and my sister's names in the grass. For several weeks during the hot summer, when the rest of the grass withered in the heat, there on the top of the hill were the lush green names: Val and Rhonda.

I owned that hill. My name proved it.

"Isn't *my* hill gorgeous with *my* name on it?" I would tease Valerie.

"My name's on it, too," she would reply.

Those were the times that I relented and called it *our* hill, but only for a time.

When I fell in love, I introduced my boyfriend to the hill, and the words "our hill" took on new meaning. In the winter, I showed him how much fun we could have sledding down the long slopes. We picked daffodils and dogwood flowers there in the spring and grapes in late summer. As our relationship matured, Dad fertilized another name in the grassy hill. But as we sat on the slope, held hands, and planned our future life together, it became quite clear that my hill would not be part of that future.

On a hot July day, I walked up my hill slowly, the pinging of the piano competing with the sounds of the songbirds. I wore a white flowing dress and my left hand held Dad's right arm. A gentle wind blew, wrapping my wedding dress around his legs.

Dad adjusted my gown and we continued our walk through the finely mowed green grass, specially manicured for this extraordinary day. We made our way to the grape arbor. There, beneath the blue sky, my future husband awaited me. My uncle, waiting to perform his first marriage ceremony, nervously watched as we approached. One hundred and fifty relatives and friends stood on my hill, looking down on our fairy-tale ceremony.

On that sacred hill, I said goodbye to my childhood and embraced my new life.

Since that day, I've lived on many hills: from a hilltop in Kentucky overlooking the Big Sandy River to a hillside in Sydney, Australia, where surfers and ships dotted the Pacific Ocean. But the hill that is most endearing in my memories is the one that I christened in my youth.

During the years that have followed my wedding, my husband and I have seen our share of valleys, but it's always our hill that brings us back to reality. It's that hill where we made our eternal vows to each other before God and where our life began as one. Long gone are the fertilized letters of our names, but our memory of that hill will always be etched in our hearts.

Do I still—many years later—cherish my hill and what its memories hold? I do.

❧

Valerie would argue that this was her story, for two years after my wedding, my sister wore a white gown and held Dad's arm as she walked up her hill toward her husband-to-be. And just like a fairy-tale ending, there on the hillside were their names, dark green and lush, for the whole world to see.

Rhonda Lane Phillips

The Wedding Ring

In 1949, through a strange sequence of events, my husband found himself pastor of a small rural church. A congregation in Lansing, Kansas, was without a minister, so the desperate bishop assigned Merris Brady—a nineteen-year-old college student who was studying to be a city manager, and who had absolutely no experience in ministering—to a congregation.

Despite the obvious obstacles, Merris agreed to help out. He quickly read the required books and obtained a preacher's license. After that, he was on his own. Apparently, the bishop thought that since Merris's father was a minister, Merris would know what to do.

Because he did not own a car, Merris hitchhiked sixty miles from his college to the church every Sunday morning. The church was a white-frame building nestled in a smattering of houses on a gravel road. The town was so small that if it hadn't been for a physician and a pharmacist, there would have been no business district at all. The only thriving enterprise—and the town's claim to fame—was the Lansing State Penitentiary.

The good people of the congregation greeted their new pastor warmly. In return, Merris preached every Sunday, met with the youth, and visited church members in the hospital. Everything sailed along just fine, until he was asked to do a wedding.

Merris suggested that the prospective bride and groom invite a real minister to perform the ceremony, but they wanted him. So, armed with a little black book that contained the order of worship for a wedding ceremony, and with all the enthusiasm of youth, Merris helped the couple plan their wedding.

On the day of the wedding, the pews filled quickly with friends and relatives. The lovely bride and the anxious groom stood with their attendants at the front of the sanctuary, facing the minister. Everything proceeded according to plan until it came time to place the ring on the bride's finger.

Prepared to have the groom repeat after him, "With this ring I thee wed," Merris reached for the ring. Whether it was Merris or the very nervous best man remains a mystery, but in the exchange, the wedding ring slipped from their fingers. As chance would have it, they were standing over a large metal grate—the only source of heat from the coal-burning furnace. If someone had carefully aimed the ring, it could not have fallen at a more ill-fated angle. The hushed audience watched in horror as the ring disappeared through the lattice and plunged into the furnace below, a slight ping reverberating in the silence. Unanimous gasps circled the sanctuary.

The best man stood dumbstruck. The bride looked ready to burst into tears and the groom's face paled. Merris, unsure what to do in a situation such as this, stood frozen like a pillar of salt. Miraculously, the mother of the bride had her wits about her. She slipped her own wedding band from her finger, stepped forward and carefully—very carefully—handed her ring to the groom. The congregation breathed a collective sigh of relief and the wedding ceremony continued as if nothing unusual had occurred.

Not long after that memorable wedding, the church trustees wisely purchased a mat to cover the furnace grate during future wedding ceremonies.

Fortunately for everyone, the bungled wedding ring fiasco did not cause permanent damage. The couple stayed happily married and Merris chose the ministry as a career.

Barbara Brady

The Trousseau

In the corner of my room sits an old cedar chest. It's mine now, but it hasn't always been. Once it belonged to my grandmother, but she's been gone now for many years. Some of the treasures it holds were hers once, and then they were my mother's. Only a few are mine. I slide my fingers across the thickly lacquered top, pushing the linen cover to the floor. I press the button latch and then strain to raise the heavy lid. Immediately that familiar strong scent of cedar entwined with musty memories slips free, trailing, twisting, and teasing us into remembering. As I lift aside the crisp, yellowing tissue paper that covers the hidden treasures, I look over my shoulder to where my mom watches from the edge of the bed. She smiles. Many of her precious items are still in that chest, and she is eager to see them once more. And to share her stories.

Soon Mother's story is spilling from her memory, as bright and golden today as it had been seventy years ago in 1932. . . . In the small village of Providence, Utah, she called to her older sister, Ella, "Hurry, Ella, help me lay the table cover."

Together they fumble with a heavy, yet delicately crocheted, white tablecloth. No sooner was it stretched across the ebony table than their mother set down newly polished candleholders and candelabra made of hand-carved pine, which had been stained with walnut, then rubbed with bacon grease. Freshly plucked autumn blossoms were woven in and around their bases and then touched up with dark strands of ivy from the brick wall beyond the house.

Anna literally shivered with excitement. She and her mother and sister were laying out the many years of handiwork that made up her wedding trousseau. She couldn't even remember how many long evenings had been spent before the open-hearth fire, stitching and sewing and quilting, to be ready for this day. Today all of their close friends would come to the house to inspect the handiwork, and she prayed everything would be perfect.

Alongside the candleholders, the women placed crisp, flat-iron–pressed pillowslips embroidered with posies and butterflies, starched linen sheets with cutaway designs, napkins, tablecloths, doilies, and furniture slipcovers. Several handsome quilts, including the red-and-white wedding ring pattern, were quilted with wool batting inside. Pillows plumped full with goose down and duck feathers were propped up on a chair nearby. Kitchen dishtowels trimmed in rick-rack and bright strips of bias tape were there also.

Near the brick fireplace stood a small, drop-leaf table covered with Anna's personal lingerie items. Each item was cut from satin and then hand stitched. The edges were trimmed in dainty satin ribbons and pieces of lace. Bed jackets, soft cotton nighties, undergarments, muslin petticoats, and other unmentionables were all made to bring excitement to the impending honeymoon—but no one spoke of those things; proper women just knew. Atop the lingerie were sentimental items of jewelry, including a gold-and-rhinestone clip-on brooch that had belonged to Anna's grandma in Germany, a string of pearls from her mother, and a square-cut ruby-red ring set in filigree, which was a gift from Ella.

Toiletry items were laid out on a table nearby. They included a gold-tone hairbrush, mirror, and comb set, a cream-toned Lucite hair keeper, and the sea-green curling iron, which so perfectly set Anna's platinum blonde hair into the waves unique to flappers. And there were finely edged cotton hankies set alongside small bottles of perfumes, powders, and tiny rounds of rouge.

Anna also had a pair of brocade pillows—stitched and then stuffed with feathers—which were the envy of everyone who had seen them. To top it all off, her mother had presented her with a small, matched set of dinnerware, soft golden-yellow in color, with tiny orange flowers all across each dish. Such sets were a luxury during the postwar years, and Anna's eyes misted over when she thought of the sacrifice it must have taken for her parents to purchase such a set.

The women filled candy dishes with peppermint taffy, pastries, cake slices, and pieces of freshly baked nut breads. A crock jug was filled with chilled grape juice to drink, and heavy bowls full of shining red apples and purple Concord grapes were placed all around the room. From somewhere in the kitchen, the elusive scent of incense made itself known.

It is always the same when Mother shares this particular story. We are transported in time. But now, as she takes a deep breath as if testing the air currents for incense, I lift the final layer of tissue from the cedar chest. I push it aside, anticipating the pleasure I experience each time I reach this point. Beneath the tissue is Mother's wedding dress. Now slightly yellowed with age and delicately fragile, it beckons to me. The fabric is ivory-hued polished cotton with straight and simple lines, except for the bow at the dropped waist. The neckline is high and modest, the sleeves long and narrow, with only a few pearl buttons and a touch of lace adding to the simplicity. Standing before the mirror, I hold the dress close, imagining myself as the bride. I catch Mother's eye and we both laugh. Never could I even dream of fitting into such a petite dress.

With trembling hands, she lifts up a narrow satin ribbon and ties it in my hair, explaining that garden flowers had made up her simple bouquet but a few blossoms were also tucked in beneath the ribbon in the hair.

How beautiful she must have been.

In my mind, I hear the guests arriving at her door. I hear her girlish laughter as my mother hurries to her room to change into a party dress while her own mother and her sister, Ella, swing open the door to welcome their guests.

"Come in," her mother says. "The trousseau is waiting—and Anna is ready."

Jean Davidson

 I Do

The bride wore pink. The layered hem of her dress hung in delicate ripples, brushing her slim legs. If she was nervous, it didn't show. A corsage of carnations and rosebuds sat jauntily below her shoulder. Her new shoes weren't broken in yet, and although she tried not to limp, I could tell her feet were hurting.

The groom could hardly take his eyes off his betrothed as she entered the room and moved gracefully into his heart. The best man, wearing a borrowed tie, stood beside him, offering moral support.

This was no ordinary wedding. The bride was seventy-eight years old, and the groom was eighty-five. Who would have ever thought I would be attending the wedding of my husband's elderly aunt—nearly twenty-five years after my own wedding!

We few attendees had been sworn to secrecy. A friend of the bride's had offered her home for the wedding. The groom's son happened to be in town on business and found he would not only be attending his father's wedding but he would operate the video recorder, as well. My husband Neil and I were the attendants.

The chaplain asked for God's blessing as we bowed our heads in prayer. He quoted from I Corinthians 13:4–8.

Love is patient, love is kind.

My mind wandered to the first time I met the bride. It was 1985, and she was in England visiting her daughter. My mother-in-law had passed away suddenly, and we had called Aunt Cora to let her know that her sister had died. She immediately made the long and arduous flight from England to Canada to be with us. Although I had never seen Aunt Cora before, I recognized her from pictures, and saw her first as we met her at the airport. "There she is!" I remember saying, with relief. She comforted us in our grief although she, too, was grieving.

It does not envy, it does not boast.

Somewhere during the years, I dropped the "Aunt" and just called her Cora. I loved her as if she was my own aunt. She lived in Florida, so we got to know each other via letters and cards. Then after a lengthy illness, her husband died.

It is not proud, it is not rude.

Neil and I often visited Cora in Florida. She endearingly introduced me to her friends as her niece, not just her nephew's wife. Actively involved in the community, sitting on various boards, and being a friend to all were the mainstays of her life.

It is not self-seeking, it is not easily angered.

Cora had known Francis for a long time. He had been widowed many years ago. Now that they were both retired, they spent time together and filled their lives with travel and cruises. I had never heard their voices raised in anything but laughter and song.

It keeps no record of wrongs.

Several weeks before we were to fly to Florida, Cora e-mailed us, mentioning a surprise, and said to be sure to bring some good clothes. As I pondered the possibilities of what the surprise could be, my husband sighed in exasperation, and said, "It's probably just a belated birthday present for you." But I knew it was something more. Why would she say to bring good clothes?

Love does not delight in evil but rejoices with the truth.

A few days before we were to leave for Florida, I had a revelation that Cora and Francis were going to get married. Neil scoffed, "Why would they marry now?" Still, my intuition told me I was right.

Love always protects, always trusts, always hopes, always perseveres.

As it turned out, no one was more surprised than Neil when Cora and Francis announced their impending nuptials. "I knew it!" I declared trium-phantly, to everyone's astonishment.

Love bears all things, believes all things, hopes all things, endures all things.

Love may be blind, but a second marriage is a real eye-opener and often the triumph of hope over experience. Cora and Francis had waited ten years to marry. We were soon to find out why.

Love never fails.

As the chaplain spoke of the seasons in marriage, the sun poured through the big living room window, bestowing its warmth and blessing. I said a silent thank you for my own blessings and for being here to witness the joining of two special hearts. My thoughts were pushed aside when I heard the age-old vows. "Do you, Francis, take this woman . . . " followed by his firm response, "I will."

Then, "Do you, Cora, take this man . . . "

"I sure will," she stated emphatically.

Francis solemnly pledged his love. "I, Francis, take you Cora, to be my wedded wife, and I do promise and covenant before God and these witnesses to be your loving and faithful husband, in plenty and in want, in joy and in sorrow, in sickness and in health, as long as we both shall live. May we endure each storm and season, and may we capture each joy."

Then it was Cora's turn; her eyes focused intently on Francis's face as she repeated the same words with conviction, eyes shining with love.

Neil handed the ring to Francis, who slipped it on his beloved's finger. "Cora, I give you this ring as a symbol of my commitment to me . . . "

We chuckled, and the chaplain smiled and said, "Are you marrying yourself? Francis has married himself!"

A little flustered, Francis made the correction to "my commitment to you" and ended up marrying

Cora after all. I handed Cora the other ring, and she completed her vows, and with those words, Francis and Cora became man and wife.

When asked why they chose to marry now, after being together for so many years, Francis grinned and teasingly said, "She passed her ten-year probationary period, so it was time!"

I smiled and fought back tears. Not only had I been blessed with an aunt whom I dearly loved, but I now also had Uncle Francis, complete with his eighty-five-year-old sense of humor. And in that instance, I knew, also, that there was more to this thing called love than that which meets the eye. At their age, they did not need to tie the knot to know they loved one another, or to prove anything to the world at large. Instead, they had done it because they wanted to reach the highest pinnacle love offers to each of us. They knew what every couple in love eventually discovers: Completing the circle of love with a ring and a vow is the only way to truly understand the contentment love offers.

As I smiled along with them on their wedding day, I finally let the tears of happiness slide unchecked down my cheeks. Like all couples before them, they had each found what they had unknowingly sought— the one thing that could make their individual worlds complete: the sanctity of marriage.

Maria Harden

My Prince Charming Wore Roller Skates

Most households do not look forward to April 15—the dreaded tax date. But in our household it's a day of celebration. It signals the end of a busy tax season for my husband, who is an accountant, and it also is the anniversary of the first time my husband and I held hands.

I remember it like it was yesterday. I was fourteen and in love. Although I had followed Terry around school for months, an embarrassing situation had prevented me from getting up the nerve to approach him. Terry was a starter for the junior varsity basketball team, and I was a cheerleader. Being nearsighted—and too vain to wear my glasses—led me to scream out another player's name instead of Terry's when he made a half-court basket in the final second of the game. The crowd recognized my mistake and my face turned crimson as my error was pointed out. I was so embarrassed. I couldn't even look at Terry as he walked toward the locker room.

I had fallen for this guy. But every time I looked at him, I remembered my blunder, as I'm sure he did. As far as I was concerned, getting Terry to notice me was an impossible task. But my best friend had other ideas. She and Terry attended the same church and she was set on playing matchmaker. Seeing her opportunity, she invited me to a church-sponsored skating party. When it came time to drive the fifteen miles to the rink, she literally pushed me into Terry's parents' car. I was so embarrassed I wanted to sink through the floorboards.

Things didn't get much better once we arrived. Each time the announcer called for a "couple skate," I prayed Terry would ask me. He didn't. Finally, I'd waited long enough. For the remainder of the afternoon, I took turns skating with Terry's two best friends. As the announcer called for the last "couple skate" of the day, Terry awkwardly skated toward me.

"I guess you wonder why I haven't asked you to couple skate," he said nervously.

Trying not to look into those big beautiful brown eyes, I glanced away nonchalantly. "No, not really," I replied.

He cast his eyes downward. "I didn't ask because I don't skate very well. If you're not afraid that I'll make you fall, would you please skate with me?"

This time I looked into those eyes and my heart melted.

As we skated, hand in hand, to "Always and Forever," I knew my life would never be the same. I'd never known a guy who would admit he had a fault or worry about a girl's feelings. This guy not only had beautiful eyes, he had a beautiful heart, and I knew I had found my Prince Charming. As we skated around the rink, I felt like Cinderella at the ball. I clung tightly to his hand—not because I was afraid of midnight, but to help keep him from falling.

Looking at our wedding pictures now, my favorite is the one where we walk down the aisle as husband and wife. After being pronounced man and wife, most couples walk down the aisle with the bride's hand tucked neatly in the crook of her husband's arm. Not us. We walked down the aisle hand in hand, the way we had seven years before in the skating rink. Today, as then, I still know that with Terry's strong hand in mine, we will not stumble and we will not fall.

Stephanie Ray Brown

 Running Late

"Hurry up, Shug," my husband, Henry, calls from the living room. "We're going to be late."

"Okaaaay," I sigh, pulling rollers from my hair as I study my reflection in the bathroom mirror. "Why is he always badgering me to hurry?" I mumble. Steel-blue eyes stare back knowingly, and my mouth curls into a smile. If he were to write a book about our marriage, it would be titled *Running Late*.

Colorful visions of 1969 flash before my eyes, as if they were just taking place that instant rather than thirty-five years earlier.

Henry—tall and handsome and thoroughly disgusted—points to the sign on the courthouse door. "This can't be right! It says: Closed for Sedalia Day so all employees can attend the Missouri State Fair." A frown creases his brow. "I wanted to get our marriage license earlier in the week, but, no, you said, 'Let's wait until Thursday.' Now we've got a problem."

"Look," I say, my hands planted firmly on my hips, "we still have time to cover the three-day waiting period. All we have to do is find a courthouse that is open somewhere."

He heaves a sigh and yanks open the passenger door of the car.

"Why are you always late?"

"I've been busy getting all the other things done," I answer, wounded by his insensitivity.

That day, we ended up driving to the town of Warrensburg, thirty miles away, to secure the license. Today, I can't help but smile. Our marriage began "running late"—how can he expect it to change now?

When our wedding day rolled around, I still wasn't quite ready.

Under the hair dryer at the beauty shop that morning, I frantically hemmed my going-away dress. Oops, almost late again!

Through the years our biggest disagreements have been over my being late. I do try to be on time, but don't manage very well, and Henry cringes whenever we are the last to walk into weddings, funerals, or any gathering.

However, he'd have to admit, there was one time when being late was a blessing. At the approach of our twenty-fifth anniversary, we talked about having a party, and since we do not have children, we knew we would have to do all the arrangements ourselves. Unfortunately, because of a string of responsibilities, beginning with my mother falling and breaking her hip, August 23 came and went. We settled for an anniversary dinner date the following Saturday evening with our close friends, Rita and Arthur.

As usual, the evening started for Henry and me with a well-intentioned, albeit impatient, comment when Henry glanced in at me and said, "Hurry up, Shug, they'll be here any minute." I was running a little late, but I quickly forged ahead, spraying my hair into a frozen state at the sound of the doorbell, and rushing into the living room.

"Come in," Henry said, holding open the front door. I moved quickly to his side.

I admit to being a little surprised when Derek, Rita and Arthur's youngest grandson, bounded into the hallway.

"If you two are ready, I'll drive," Arthur said. "We need to drop Derek off at his house first."

"Isn't Rita coming in?" I asked.

"She's waiting in the car. She figured we would want to get going. You know how crowded places get on a Saturday night in Sedalia."

It didn't take long to travel the short distance to Derek's two-story white house.

"They've got lots of company," I noted as we came around the corner.

"Oh—those cars?" Rita turned around from the front seat, dismissing them with a wave of her hand. "Greg and Dawn are having a class reunion."

It wasn't until we pulled into the driveway that I saw the sign: "Congratulations, Henry and Linda, on your 25th anniversary."

Derek jumped out of the car, clapping his hands. "Surprise!"

We were surprised. We stumbled out of the car in a state of shock at the sight filling the yard. About 150 friends, young and old, shouted, "Happy anniversary!" We both blinked back tears amid hugs and well wishes.

"Here's the cake," Greg and Dawn's youngest daughter, Holly, shouted while skipping ahead, her feet barely touching the ground. "Grandma Rita made it."

Henry squeezed my hand as we were ushered toward a three-layer wedding cake complete with blue flowers and columns—an exact replica of our wedding cake.

Greg and Dawn's oldest daughter, Valerie, shouted, "Look over here!" We followed her to another table where a guest book and a bouquet of white carnations waited. "Grandma Ellen crocheted the basket for the flowers," Valerie explained.

"Let's go eat," Dawn said as she handed each of us a plate.

Henry stared at the assortment of food. "My gosh!" He shook his head. "I can't believe this."

I smile at the memory, then startle as my husband interrupts my thoughts.

"Shug!" Henry says loudly in my ear, his finger tapping me on the shoulder. "Quit your daydreaming. We have to leave in ten minutes."

"Okay," I say guiltily, removing the last roller from my hair. I grab the comb, tease my hair quickly, and then spray until I have created a hairstyle in a slightly less frozen state than it was in 1969. I glance at the clock and continue with my makeup.

This year we would celebrate our thirty-fifth anniversary. Since we said the words "I do," we have learned to overlook the things that bug us, to appreciate our differences, to support and encourage. And, most important, we've learned that love never fails.

I cock my head to listen for the words I know Henry will shout next. I am not disappointed. In a moment, I hear his voice reverberate from the kitchen, "I'm going out to start the car." I smile and hurry to finish. It's good to know that some things will always be the same: I will always be a tad late, and Henry will always be a tad impatient.

Linda Kaullen Perkins

Under the Cottonwood Tree

Only a 12-foot trunk, devoid of bark and sun-bleached to a gray-white, remains of the once magnificent cottonwood tree. Yet, each time I pass it, I think back to that wonderful summer of 1974, when beneath its branches my life was forever altered.

The story began when I moved back to my hometown of Lingle, Wyoming, following a series of misadventures that had left me emotionally shattered. I came home, knowing that I would find the peace and support that I needed to heal my wounded soul.

Not long after returning to Lingle, I sat in my car at a stop sign, waiting for the traffic to clear. A green car, driven by a girl with fire-red hair—the reddest I've ever seen—drove by. As she passed, I thought to myself, "There goes the girl I'm going to marry."

One major problem stood in my way: I didn't know her name.

Not long after that chance encounter, I got a telephone call asking me to sing for the funeral of an elderly resident. The original singer had suddenly become ill. I was told that the organist would be a newcomer to town named Kathy (coincidentally, also a replacement for an ailing organist). Since we had never worked together, I decided to contact her to arrange a rehearsal. I could scarcely believe my fortune when I recognized the lady at the organ as my dream girl—the redhead with the green car.

After the funeral, I made several attempts to contact Kathy but met with no success. Neither of us had telephones. And messages always seemed to get delayed. Then, one day, my job took me to a farmhouse just outside town. As I worked in the yard, a familiar green car pulled into the driveway. Unbeknownst to me, my red-headed friend had moved into a small house on the same property.

I knew immediately that I needed to act if I hoped to make her my wife, but my financial situation had taken a significant turn for the worse and I had no money for a proper date. So I did what seemed like the right thing to do at the time—I lied. I approached Kathy with a tale of a picnic at my house the following Sunday. Since I didn't want to frighten her off with thoughts of an afternoon alone at the home of a strange man, I told her that I had friends coming over, and asked her to join us. She accepted.

I couldn't have been happier. However, I then found myself faced with the dilemma of finding some friends who could come and make my story a reality.

Sunday afternoon arrived, and so did Kathy. I had planned to barbeque hamburgers, so I had the charcoal lit and ready. I borrowed a picnic table from my parents, which I placed in the shade of the huge cottonwood tree that graced my backyard. We walked and talked our way through the garden as we waited for my friends to arrive (surprisingly, I had succeeded in conscripting a couple to legitimize my invitation). My friends, however, forgot about the invitation, and didn't get there until nearly two hours later.

When they arrived, I got the grill going again for the burgers. Unfortunately, Kathy was quite the distraction. The finished product looked more like the charcoal briquettes than anything edible. Then, to add the final humiliation, my majestic cottonwood chose that particular moment to begin dropping its seed. The gentle breeze that filled the air that afternoon was so thick with fluffy cottonwood seeds that we couldn't take a bite without getting a mouthful of sticky cotton.

Once the day ended, I resigned myself to the idea that Kathy would probably never go out with me again, but I decided to try again, anyway. To my surprise, she accepted another date—and then another. By summer's end, we knew that we were meant to be together, and when I asked her to marry me there was no hesitation.

On a beautiful Saturday afternoon, just three short months after that disastrous first date, Kathy and I again stood in the shade of the cottonwood tree, and in the presence of family and friends, she became my wife.

As the ceremony progressed, a couple of acquaintances who were delivering a new clothes dryer to my neighbor set their load down, walked to the fence behind where we stood, and watched. When the pastor pronounced us husband and wife, we were surprised by applause. To make the day complete, Kathy's ten-year-old nephew appointed himself the official photographer, and added colorful commentary as he captured our first kiss.

"Oh, yuck!" he shouted. "He's kissin' her!"

Today—thirty years, three children, and six grandchildren later—the memory of events blessed by the cottonwood's shade still brighten our lives. We remain together, as happy now as we were then.

Bob Rose

Momma Throws a Wedding

John and I tied the knot in a small ceremony, followed by a wonderful luncheon with both sets of parents and John's sister's family, at the ritzy Park Schenley restaurant. After lunch, my parents hugged us and, with tears in their eyes, departed for the airport. We would be returning to Carnegie Tech on Monday morning and had arranged to spend the weekend at my new in-laws' home.

Although the wedding and luncheon had been wonderful, my heart ached for a real reception with lots of people sharing our happy occasion with us.

While Momma and I were preparing dinner that night, I'm not sure if I wore my heart on my sleeve, or if my new mother-in-law was just that perceptive, but I could have burst into tears when she asked, "Wouldn't you like a real party? Not just with us, but with the whole family?" She made a well in the flour and broke three large eggs into the indentation and then glanced back up at me.

"Really?" I asked, my voice barely a whisper. "I would, if it wouldn't be too much trouble."

A smile lit her face. "Say no more," she replied. Moving her calloused hands gently, she mixed the egg with the flour and formed dough. "Watch closely," she said as she rolled it out. Then she winked. "I won't always be there to show you what to do. Now you try." She handed me the pliable ball of dough and smiled as I kneaded it. "Not that hard. It's done nothing to you," she added.

I laughed. "Think I'll ever learn?"

"You can do physics. Why not noodles?"

"It isn't only cooking I don't know, it's all those other things," I confided as I wiped off my hands on the apron, flecks of gooey dough streaking the crisp white cotton.

She gave me the longest hug and then said. "Look. You're my daughter now, same as if I gave birth to you. Give yourself time. You'll learn fine."

I stood there, letting my senses fill with the love from her touch. "Thanks, Momma. I love you, too."

"What do you want for your wedding party?" she asked. "Supper or cake and coffee?"

"Supper with cake sounds wonderful, but I don't want you to fuss," I said, not wanting to impose.

"It's no bother. You're part of our family." She pinned a gray strand of hair back into the braids wrapped around her head, readjusted her glasses, and smiled at me. Her blue eyes shone and her cheeks glowed.

Momma threw a real wedding celebration that Sunday, the likes of which John and I shall never forget. John's relatives were all there, and the table was filled to overflowing.

My eyes filled with tears when I walked into the room and saw the carefully decorated cake, topped with a ceramic bride and groom, surrounded by gifts. Momma's yellow Art Deco Formica table, bought at a fire sale, was covered with service platters, heaped to overflowing. The house literally exploded with wonderful aromas—memorable scents that welcomed guests and comforted children.

Over dinner, bites of food were interspersed with family tales, gossip, and good wishes. With our crazy schedule, cooking was my lowest priority, and I hadn't realized what we were missing.

Soon it was time to open the presents. All the gifts were beautiful and appreciated, but it was the last gift—the one Momma gave us—that I will cherish forever.

"Don't wash it or you'll ruin the finish," she said as I opened the box and pulled out an iron skillet.

"Scrub it out with salt if it gets dirty, and it will never stick." She smiled happily, the look on her face one of total acceptance. She nodded to Papa and smiled. "My mother gave it to me when we got married."

I looked around the room at all the loving faces, and at my mother-in-law, who had called me her own daughter. Then I looked at the figurine on the top of the cake and closed my eyes. There was no doubt that this was where I belonged.

Rhoda Novak

A Lasting Affair

Southern weddings, at least in my family, aren't about long white dresses, magnolias, and formal gatherings. Rather, they are about everlasting love.

My grandmother, Melba Creech, grew up in Wendell, North Carolina, a small town near Raleigh. My grandfather, Julian Williford, and his kin lived in Lizard Lick—a tiny town whose citizens went to Wendell for fun and supplies. As Lizard Lick doesn't have much more than a general store, Julian and Melba only saw one another at church outings, and then once again when Melba's thirteen brothers and sisters came home for a family reunion, but it didn't take long for the two teenagers to fall in love.

With more dreams than money, the young lovers decided to get married. Imagine a street scene from

Mayberry, and you'll understand why it was a bit of a production when Julian drove Melba to town one day and sought out the preacher. They found him working at the gas station, and were married right there in the service bay.

Some years later, Melba gave birth to their second child and first daughter, Gloria, whom they called Dene. Destined to follow in her parents' footsteps, Dene met and fell in love with a handsome young man during her high school years. Upon hearing the news, Melba announced that she was going to throw a big, fancy wedding for Dene, and her beau, Eddie Collins, the likes of which she had never had—but Dene had other plans. On Dene's eighteenth birthday, she and Eddie took matters into their own hands. They would be married, and it would be this day!

They told their families they were going to the beach. They quickly packed everything they would need for the ceremony into Eddie's old car and headed due east. When they were out of sight from prying eyes, they turned sharply toward the south and crossed the state line.

They were married at The Wedding Chapel, in Dillon, South Carolina—a place not easily forgotten by anyone who has traveled Interstate 95 through the Carolinas. "South of the Border" is Dillon's claim to fame. Even today it is comparatively unpopulated and sprinkled with entertaining highway signs such as: "YOU HAVE NEVER SEEN SAUSAGE A PLACE," and "KEEP YELLING KIDS, THEY'LL STOP."

In the fifties, The Wedding Chapel was known as a place for quickie marriages for the soldiers at Fort Bragg and had something of an unsavory reputation.

It was understandable then, that fur flew when the happily married couple returned home. Not only had they married in such a hurried and unorthodox manner, but they had spoiled all of Melba's wedding plans. They were immediately banished to live with Eddie's mother. But time passed, tempers cooled, and the family was reunited. And Dene and Eddie's marriage lasted, as did Julian and Melba's.

My husband, Al, and I continued the family tradition of being married in odd ways when we stood up after a Sunday morning church service and exchanged our vows. We've been incredibly happy ever since.

These are the family stories I like to share with our five children, Carole, Christy, James, Ian, and Michael. We've always laughed at the image of their proper great-grandmother getting married in a gas station, and at the thought of their grandparents running away to South of the Border (of all places!). Perhaps our children even laugh when they think of the manner in which their own parents tied the knot. But I know one thing for certain: As our children grow and mature and think about their own marriages, they will remember that these are the kind of marriages that last and last and last.

Suzanne Cherry

Faithful Pie

If my father is to be believed, he fell in love with my mother over a slice of lemon pie.

Whenever he tells the story of how he came to love my mother, my mother quietly says, "Pshaw," when he gets to the part about the lemon pie. She doesn't believe in love at first sight, but when my father looks at my mother with light in his eyes, it's quite apparent that he does.

My father has always been hardheaded. It seems perfectly natural to me that a small-town boy from upstate South Carolina ended up out in Wyoming pumping gas for a living in 1973, while his college friends enjoyed the deferment that came with being matriculated students at the University of South Carolina. Dad had been among them a few years before—shooting for grades just low enough to get his own father's attention and just high enough to keep him out of Vietnam. In one of those last attempts to grab a different sort of life, he packed up his Fairlane and drove out to Wyoming, finally stopping at Old Faithful, deep within Yellowstone National Park.

Dad had been working at the filling station that overlooked the geyser for over a year. In late spring, the summer hires, wanting a taste of the Wild West, moved in to help combat the flux of tourists. My mother was among them. She was assigned a waitress job at the old Hamilton store, a general store that catered to tourists but had a lunch counter where tourists and locals alike could get a burger and Coke and—according to my father—one heck of a slice of pie. The store had a second floor, and my mother was walking downstairs in her starched yellow gingham uniform when my father spotted her for the first time. He'd almost finished his lunch, but after he saw my mother, he ordered another slice of pie just so he'd have something to say to her.

That was the beginning. For Dad, it was love at first sight. My mother took her time, falling in love slowly as they began to spend evenings together. They would drive the fifty miles outside the Park to the little town of Gardiner, Montana, where they could share a pizza and a long talk on the way home. When she called home to her parents, she talked about a boy with long hair and a beard, a hippie without a cause, a learned man without an education. All of this made my grandparents very uneasy.

As the summer nights became shorter, the tourist traffic slowed. My mother was to return to her senior year at the University of Michigan. This prompted my father, in the typical haste that only young love can produce, to recklessly propose and my bewildered mother to accept. He gave her his mother's engagement ring, and in return she slipped the small gold ring that had been her grandmother's off her finger and onto the chain that hung around his neck.

My mother returned to Ann Arbor and settled into her old life, except now everything was different and the certainty of married life loomed. Dad wanted to stay in Gardiner, and my mother wondered what she'd do in the wintry off-season. All around her, friends were going to law school, working on Capitol Hill, traveling to Europe. Was she really going to be the wife of a filling station attendant in Montana? That winter, she gave my father back the ring.

Years passed. My mother did all of the things that she'd feared missing out on. She interned on Capitol Hill and spent two years teaching in rural Australia. Only occasionally did she wonder about the long-haired boy from South Carolina who'd landed by chance at the Old Faithful filling station. My father, however, did wonder about my mother. In fact, he wondered about her so much that he forced himself to try to forget her. He drove back to South Carolina and the little town he'd grown up in. And while he was busy trying to forget about my mother, he ran into an old childhood friend who was not my mother, and for a while that felt right and so he married her.

They made a life together, and Dad returned to school and worked at being a good husband, but just friendship in a marriage isn't enough. One day, his wife said she didn't want to be married to a friend— she wanted more—and my father agreed. So they parted as friends and began the inevitable division of belongings that separated out the three years that they had been together.

And so it was that one day, when my father was up in the attic sorting through old boxes, something clanged to the floor. It was my mother's ring, the one he'd worn around his neck as a promise years before. He looked at it in the light and knew that wherever my mother was, she'd mourn its loss. He packaged the ring carefully and sent it to her parents' address with a note attached for her.

Not long after, my father received a letter in his mailbox with a Boston postmark that he didn't recognize. In it, he found my mother's handwriting, thanking him for remembering the ring and returning it to her. But she didn't just ask about the ring. She asked about the weather and his family and the marriage he'd lost. And all her asking gave my father hope.

For months, they wrote back and forth, filling each other in on what had happened during the years they had been apart. Finally, my father explained that he wanted to make the long drive to Boston to see my mother again.

When he saw her for the first time in so long, he says it was just like that first time she served him that slice of lemon pie, which had tasted better than any piece he'd had before or since. And when he left Boston later that week to make the long drive back home, my mother was sitting in the seat beside him.

Rachel Beanland

. . . And Still Holding

Colorful balloon bouquets bobbed their Valentine greetings from each table, and strands of metallic garland portraying arrow-armed Cupids adorned the walls. Silverware clattered and glasses clinked while the crowd of old friends—and some newer ones—gathered in the hall reserved for this big event. The melodic, mellow piano notes of "The Anniversary Waltz" wove through the air, creating a romantic ambiance.

It was an ideal setting for a first anniversary celebration—the same place they'd held the wedding a year earlier. The facility was humble yet homey; frugal but festive.

Everyone looked up and began clapping when the guests of honor entered. Norma, petite and radiant in a crimson dress, glided in. At her elbow, courtly long-limbed Fred—always the Southern gentleman—

leaned low to catch her expression when she first caught sight of the room. The wide smile that lit her face brought an equally broad smile to his lips.

And the partying began.

The room resounded with giggling and grins, teasing and toasts. Sipping a sparkling drink, Norma sat contentedly in her chair, watching the festivities and visiting with friends. Fred, always the more social, outgoing, and fun-loving of the two, slowly made his way from table to table.

He accepted congratulations.

"We do make an ideal couple, don't we?" he agreed. "After all, Norma robbed the cradle . . . and I always did have an attraction to older women!" Everyone hooted.

He shared their romance.

"Why, we met one Fourth of July. We both showed up to watch the fireworks," he arched an eyebrow, "and then created a few of our own." A few people giggled.

But even while he sparkled in the spotlight, Fred kept an eye on Norma. As a result, it wasn't long before he noticed she had begun to droop with fatigue. After a year of marriage, he was more solicitous than ever. In only a few strides, he was at her side.

"Now I get you to myself, Sweetheart," Fred said as he patted Norma's creped hand. "We'll let the others continue celebrating our anniversary."

Tenderly tucking the worn lap robe around her thin thighs, he freed the side brakes and began pushing her wheelchair down the corridor toward their room.

"Cradle-robbing" ninety-year-old Norma fingered the anniversary strand of pearls hanging slack around her wattled neck, ducked her head flirtatiously, and slid a coquettish smile upward—at her eighty-nine-year-old groom—as he escorted her out.

"Yep. One year and holding." Fred looked over his shoulder at the other nursing home residents. "And to think," he added, "our kids said it would never last!"

Carol McAdoo Rehme

Going to the Fireworks

The other day, the traffic was slow and my husband was becoming impatient. As he began to grumble, I recalled a traditional family saying. Smiling, I leaned close and murmured, "John and Martha, going to the fireworks." He immediately laughed and took my hand. Then he slowed down and began pointing out things to the kids that perhaps only he could see. He kept them busy looking for large boulders rubbed smooth by the buffalo, and black-nosed badgers with silver backs that were holed up in dens along the way. When we finally arrived at our destination, my daughter looked at me with her brow furrowed.

"Who are John and Martha?"

In her innocent face, I saw the face of another child: me. On family car rides when I was young, there were occasions when the whole line of cars on the road slowed to a snail's pace. Usually this was because someone in the front of the line—perhaps driving an antiquated vehicle—was oblivious to anyone else as he drove along enjoying the scenery. Sometimes when that happened, my father's vocabulary changed, and seldom-heard curse words were mumbled under his breath. Mother would smile patiently and whisper, "John and Martha, going to the fireworks."

Whenever she uttered that phrase, my father visible relaxed. He'd squeeze Mother's hand, drape an arm around her shoulders, and pull her close. Then he'd point to the large boulders in the wheat fields and explain that they had been rubbed smooth by the buffalo that once roamed across the Great Plains. Daddy said if we looked real hard we could see brown bits of fur snagged on the edges. Driving slowly along, he'd point out other interesting things like black-nosed badgers hiding in their dens.

Sometimes, I'd look up and catch Dad sneaking a kiss from Mom. Once when he caught me spying, he quickly shouted, "There he is!" Soon my attention was riveted back to the elusive badger and his den.

As my husband drove down the road slowly, my mind wandered, and my daughter grew fidgety. The wistful smile on my face did nothing to explain who John and Martha were, and just like me at that same age, she wanted an answer. To appease her, I told her the story my mother had told me so long ago.

In the days of my grandparents, there was a couple of young lovers named John and Martha, who lived on the prairies. John loved Martha very much, and though he could talk to her younger brothers and sisters with no problem, he was so tongue-tied around Martha he couldn't speak. When it was announced that there would be a Fourth of July fireworks display in a neighboring town, John got up the courage to ask Martha's father if he could take her. Her father agreed to the escort. John was on cloud nine! When he came to pick Martha up in his wagon, he figured he'd have her all to himself for a change, but he was wrong. After helping Martha up onto the seat, he heard giggling. There, in the back of the wagon, sat Martha's younger siblings.

The trip was terribly short between the towns, and John knew that the only way to make his time with Martha last was to travel at a snail's pace and let the other wagons pass. The short trip turned into a two-hour drive. John walked his horses slowly, letting other buggies pass by. Nearly all the drivers had scowls on their faces, but John didn't mind. He only had eyes for Martha.

Martha's siblings began to whine as the time dragged on, so John kept them occupied with tales of pixies in the long grass. When they tired of that story, he explained that if they watched carefully they might see the black nose and silvery back of a badger off to the right where it lay hidden in its den. As John wove his tallest tales, Martha edged closer to him on the seat. Somewhere during that long drive, she took his hand in hers and he kissed it.

When they got to the fireworks, the children told their father about the badger den and the pixies. Their father smiled and shook his head, and Martha's mother winked at him knowingly. John and Martha found a spot a few feet away from the rest of her family that night, and as the sky lit up John proposed to Martha. With fireworks glowing in her eyes, and John's hand held firmly in her own, Martha accepted.

As my story came to a close, my daughter's eyes filled with longing, and I could tell she hoped that John and Martha were her great-grandparents. I hugged her tightly. I had long hoped the same thing. When I was a child my grandparents were always quick to spin a yarn about pixies in the tall grass, and I, just like my daughter, fell for it every time.

Nancy J. Bennett

A Magic
Wedding Dress

"I can't afford a stunning wedding dress," I wailed to my mother.

I was heartbroken. Every bride wants to wear the perfect gown on her wedding day, and I simply could not settle for anything less than a magical gown. But Glenn and I had put off our marriage ceremony once already because I couldn't afford the dress of my dreams, and I was very concerned that Glenn was beginning to think me fickle. To make matters worse, my father's thoughts headed the same way.

"Garnet," he said, "Glenn may think you're hard to please. Surely you can decide on a wedding dress."

But I could not. I wanted magic and as of yet had not found it.

Before I could burst into tears again, Mother quickly stepped forward and announced that she would make the dress of my dreams for me. I was only too pleased to accept her offer.

We immediately went shopping and returned home laden down with yards and yards of satin and tulle and plenty of lace to cover up any mistakes that occurred. We also purchased small silk roses for accenting the skirt, a variety of ribbon, many kinds of thread, and four wedding dress patterns.

As soon as we had taken the material into Mother's sewing room and spread our purchases on the cutting table, we heard a knock on the front door. When Mother opened the door, our neighbor, Pearl Howerton, poked her head inside. "Peggy told me you were going to make Garnet's wedding dress," she said. "Can I help?"

Mrs. Howerton, the best seamstress in Doniphan, had been sewing the community women's and children's clothes for thirty or more years. Who better could have knocked on the door at this crucial time?

Mother smiled wide. "Pearl, you are an angel!"

In no time at all, Mother had guided Pearl toward the sewing room. After looking at our supplies, they cast their eyes on me and demanded that I write down exactly what I wanted on my wedding dress and then to sketch a design.

As soon as I was finished, Pearl took the four wedding dress patterns and created the exact pattern

I wanted. Together, Mother, Pearl, and I cut, clipped, and sewed on both the sewing machine and by hand until we had an attractive, artistic, and striking wedding dress. It was like no other in the world!

As we sat there admiring it, Pearl looked at me and smiled. "My string of pearls has been broken for years. I'll never string them. I'm going to give you one as a wedding gift."

After I thanked her, I added that Glenn had given me a string of pearls with a garnet at the center as a wedding gift.

Mother clapped her hands in glee! "Somewhere on the gown let's place Pearl's pearl and a garnet. That will show who made the dress!"

It was a great idea, but when Pearl argued that my mother must also add her name to the wedding dress, Mother dug her heels in. "No," she exclaimed. "I'm not a precious stone."

Pearl thought about it a moment and then said, "Oma, you embroider an 'O' on the right front skirt where a pocket would be. Then we'll put two garnets and a pearl inside the circle and add three tiny silk roses."

I blinked back tears. I couldn't think of a more beautiful and appropriate way to include these two special women on my wedding day.

"That will be great!' I exclaimed. I smiled at Pearl and then turned toward my mother. Already, she had begun sorting her embroidery threads. She laid the milk-white strands of embroidery thread against the ivory satin of the gown to check the coordination of the whites, followed by the chalk-white thread, then the snow-white, lily-white, and oyster-white thread to match with the wedding dress material.

The 'O', the pearl, and the garnets invited respect from my friends, but the two most important men in my life—my father and Glenn—granted their hardy approval with the one comment I longed to hear: "Gosh, you'll wear a magic wedding dress!"

Garnet Hunt White

Flying to the Altar

Every little girl dreams of the beautiful white gown, the endless flowing veil, and hours of dancing until the sun rises. My great-aunt Madeline was no exception. As she watched her older sisters walk down the marble cathedral aisles in Philadelphia, she fantasized about what her own wedding dress would one day look like. But Aunt Madge was not destined to have a proper, big-city Philadelphia wedding.

In 1935, she met and fell in love with Bill, a charmingly handsome blue-eyed boy in her class— the two sat next to each other on their first day of high school. After that, they never parted, not even after their graduation in 1939. One day in the summer of 1942, on their way home from the New Jersey seashore, Bill and Madge drove past the Piper Club airfield. Bill turned the car around, drove in, and asked a pilot to take them flying. As they soared above the cornfields that glowed rose in the warm light of the setting sun, Bill asked Madge to be his wife.

She accepted and began planning the big event.

But as the shadow of World War II continued to grow, Bill joined the Army Air Corps and became a pilot. Madge promised to wait for him—after all, she wanted to walk down that aisle in true style, and planning big weddings took time! A year later, Bill was stationed in Glendale, Arizona, when he received orders to ship out to the front. It was then that Madge realized the white dress and the champagne were not as important as she once had thought. She boarded a train to Phoenix the next day.

That evening Bill was to fly training missions, so he left her a note asking her to stand outside the barracks where he lived. Madge had no idea why he would ask such a thing, but willingly complied. When she saw the B-24 rumbling low over the rooftops at sunset, with the left wing tilted down in salute, she jumped and waved, laughing and blowing kisses to Bill as he roared past in the rose-streaked sky.

Later that evening, Bill ran home from the air-field and changed into his dress uniform, and he and Madge jumped into his car and barreled down the road. By the time they reached the tiny church of St. Mary's in Glendale, it was 10:30. They knocked softly on the rectory door, hoping to find someone still awake. A jolly Franciscan priest appeared and welcomed them inside. Happy to marry two people so obviously in love, the priest ushered them up the bare wooden aisle to the top step of the tiny altar. And with no music, no flowers, and no white satin gown, a portly priest in a brown robe and sandals joined their souls together.

Today, when I ask her if she would change anything about their wedding, she laughs softly and continues rocking in her chair. And, sometimes, when she looks off into the distance, it's as if she's seeing, once again, the fading light of a rosy sunset glinting off the tilted wing of a B-24.

Michelle Ciarlo-Hayes

Off-Road Experience

I began planning our spring nuptials soon after our autumn engagement. With limited finances and a love of sewing, I decided to make my own wedding gown. Unfortunately, my mom's secondhand no-name sewing machine wasn't up to the task of handling yards of delicate, wispy fabrics.

When my soon-to-be-husband offered to buy me a new sewing machine for Christmas, I thought it was a great idea. We spent a pleasant day machine shopping—comparing the latest styles, capabilities, and prices. I was impressed with a top-of-the-line Sears Kenmore Zig Zag Model 1422. With its special settings and attachments, satin stitching, button-holes, shell edging, and putting in zippers would be a breeze. I wasn't with Don on the day he made the purchase, but I was sure that he knew just what I wanted.

While waiting for Christmas and the arrival of my new machine, I chose a pattern, purchased yards and yards of satin, tulle and lace, and dreamed of wearing my beautiful wedding gown.

On Christmas morning, Don came to my parents' house. As we exchanged numerous small gifts, the anticipation built. I couldn't wait for my big gift. Finally, Don slid a bulky bundle across the floor toward me. I tore off the colorful Christmas paper, pretending for the sake of my family that I didn't know what the gift could be. I unveiled a hard plastic case. Sears was engraved on the handle.

With much ado, I dramatically unsnapped the sides of the case, lifted the lid and . . . gasped! Inside was a genuine Singer Sewing Machine, circa 1895! A red-and-white *Sold* tag dangled from the spool threader. As I sat—wide-eyed and slack-jawed—Don enthusiastically explained the features of this state-of-the-art machine.

"It's an original Vibrating Shuttle," he said. "It doesn't just sew; it also braids, ruffles, shirrs, puffs, and quilts." Smiling into my eyes, he added, "I also got you a wrought-iron treadle sewing cabinet to put it in. It will take getting used to, but you'll soon get the hang of it—just like my grandmother did."

With its black enamel and gold filigree designs, the Singer was a princely machine—and I was ready to crown Don with it. I stared at my fiancé, whose future status with me was now in question, trying to look appreciative.

Unable to contain their mirth any longer, my family began to laugh, and Don quickly retrieved the brand new Kenmore Zig Zag machine from his car. While the Singer—his grandmother's vintage machine—was relegated to the attic, I did use the wrought-iron treadle sewing cabinet after Don refurbished it to accommodate the Kenmore.

I made my wedding dress with the new sewing machine. Later, I used it to make accessories for our home and clothes for our children. Today the Zig Zag sewing machine enjoys a second life with our grown daughters.

A few years after we were married, my prankster man struck again. On several occasions I had spoken of the fun it would be to own an off-road Jeep, preferably red. We could use it to ride the woodland trails that surrounded our home. But with three toddlers and a mortgage, I thought my dream fell on deaf ears. Not so!

On Christmas morning my husband stood next to the Christmas tree, a thread of blue yarn dangled from his hand and snaked out the door. He handed the yarn to me.

"What's this?" I asked.

He grinned slyly. "Follow it."

Taking up the challenge, I followed the blue trail through the living room, into the kitchen and out onto the porch. The yarn trail continued across the lawn, leading to the driveway where it wound in front of our green van and disappeared behind it. I held my breath. It can't be! Can it? Was it?

Sure enough, parked in the driveway was a Jeep—a two-seater with knobby tires and a roll bar. It was orange, not red, but that didn't matter. At nearly ten inches in length, it was a vehicle any self-respecting Barbie doll would be proud to drive, and, with the help of our little girls, my childhood Barbie doll did just that!

The Jeep has held up well over the years. And just as I had hoped, it has given us plenty of off-road family experiences. These days, our granddaughters' dolls spin about the backyard in my well-loved Jeep, the shine in their eyes no less bright than that which shone in mine the day I discovered the Jeep at the end of a long blue thread.

Judyann Grant

Worth the Risk

Rex and Pat Mitchell met in 1945, as World War II was ending, and married two years later. Like many couples from Memphis, they tied the knot in the small town of Hernando, Mississippi, known in the area as the wedding town. They have been married for fifty-eight years and have never regretted their decision, despite the risks they had to tackle.

"I was a nursing student with Methodist Hospital in Memphis and I lived in the dorm," said Pat. "At that time, the rules were so strict that female students weren't allowed to be married. We were allowed only one night's leave during a month and had to be in at eleven on Saturday nights and by ten on Sunday."

One fateful night, everything changed.

"I was with a friend," Rex explained. "We were going to go to the movies, but it was raining and we were broke, so I said let's go over to the USO."

When Rex spotted Pat standing with a group of friends, he moved across the dance floor to speak with her. Before he knew it, he had become enchanted with her Southern accent and pretty face.

"After that, every chance I had, I'd catch the bus from Millington and ride into town to see her after work," he explained. "Since she had to be in by seven or so, that didn't give us much time. It wasn't easy to date, but we'd sit out on a bench in front of the school until she had to go in. We were broke, but so was everyone else, so we didn't know the difference."

On that bench, the idea of marriage arose. It never crossed their minds to question the idea despite the circumstances. As soon as they had the money, they would take the plunge. When Rex finally got his dis- charge money—all at once—they had one thought: They were rich enough to get married! But because getting married was against hospital rules, they told only their families about their plans. Knowing that the Hernando newspaper didn't publish weddings, they rode the bus to Hernando on March 13, 1947, and were married immediately.

Rex laughed. "I think I might have had two or three hundred dollars, but that was enough. I bought a suit and a ring."

"The only other person who knew was my room- mate—if other people knew, they never said any- thing," said Pat. "I was all dressed up in a gray outfit with a corsage. We didn't want to be married by a Justice of the Peace, so they found a Methodist minister to marry us. It was kind of funny. Even though Rex had just been discharged from the U.S. military, he had to call his mother from the courthouse to make sure it was okay for us to get married, because we were both only nineteen!"

After Rex's parents gave their consent, the marriage took place, and the happy couple grabbed the next bus back to Memphis so Pat could get to class on time.

"I made reservations at the Gayoso Hotel for that night and when we were done with school and work, we had a seafood dinner and then stayed at the hotel," Rex recalled, shaking his head fondly at the memory. "No one ever asked us about it, but I worked with some great guys who did something I'll never forget. When I came in the next day, there was a wooden box sitting on my desk. When I opened it, I found silver settings. We never knew who gave it to us, but I knew it was one of my friends."

According to Pat and Rex, love really does conquer all. Despite being married, the two did what had to be done. Pat returned to the dorm and Rex became an apprentice printer and rented a nearby room so they could be close. It wasn't until much later that Pat realized Rex was living on bread and peanut butter, while she had plenty to eat at the dorm.

Pat grinned. "We lived apart until I graduated in 1948. I was class president and it was just better to obey the rules. It wouldn't have looked good for the president to get thrown out of school! I graduated and got my RN on a Sunday, and reported to work on Monday at Methodist Hospital. I filled out the papers with my new name and no one ever said a word to me."

Considering the risks involved, I wondered why they hadn't just waited until Pat graduated from school. But when asked, Rex replied with a soft smile. "I just had to be with her. We just couldn't wait."

Pat agreed. "We never considered any of it a sacrifice. It's just what it took. Although we were both young, we were stable even then. Maybe it's because we both came from small towns and had a strong work ethic—it all just fit together like a jigsaw puzzle."

Karen Ott Mayer

The Covered Bridge

It was cold that day in January as Chase dashed to his poetry class on the Ohio University campus. With so many old brick roads and steep hills on the way, getting there on time was a challenge, but he made it. Out of breath, he grabbed a seat in the back.

A beautiful brunette in the front of the class hadn't seen Chase arrive, but when the professor said his name, she sat straight up in her chair. "Chase Cameron," Elizabeth whispered. She liked the way the name sounded.

Letting her imagination run, the words Mrs. Chase Cameron slid across her mind. She smiled. Mrs. Elizabeth Cameron sounded pretty good, too, she thought.

Later that evening in her dorm, Elizabeth verbalized her thoughts to the three girls who shared her room, explaining that she had heard her future husband's name that day in class.

"Really?" They asked. "What's he look like?"

"I dunno," Elizabeth responded dreamily, to the surprise and laughter of her friends. "I just know I liked his name."

During the next class, when Elizabeth finally did turn around and see Chase, she was pleased with what she saw. He was six-foot-four-inches tall and had dark hair and big brown eyes. Within weeks, Chase and Elizabeth were meeting at the campus coffee shop to do homework together. They were both just getting over painful breakups and were not anxious to get serious right away, but things have a way of changing, and one spring evening they both had a change of heart.

While Elizabeth was visiting Chase's family in the country, he took her on a long drive down the back roads. Elizabeth, being from the city, loved the change of scenery. As they traveled up and down winding country roads, the view was laden with soft-rolling hills, trickling streams, old barns, cows, and horses. As the sun was going down they came upon the most serene setting: a faded white country church, its steeple still pointing tall and proud, with the gravel road curving around and into an old covered bridge. As they approached the graffiti-covered bridge, a romantic song began to play on the radio.

Chase stopped the car just outside the bridge opening. Leaving the headlights on, he turned and looked at Elizabeth. "Would you like to dance?"

What girl wouldn't love this? Elizabeth thought, as her heart melted.

Two and a half years later, at the end of their junior year, Chase felt ready to ask Elizabeth's father for her hand in marriage. With the blessings of her parents, and their promise to keep his secret, he bought the ring and then started planning his romantic request. One evening, prior to fall class enrollment, he asked his parents to help him create a romantic birthday surprise for Elizabeth, and they agreed. On the evening of Elizabeth's birthday, heavy rains pelted the state of Ohio. Chase's parents and grandmother tried to talk him out of his elaborate plan.

"Just propose to her at a romantic dinner," Chase's father suggested. "She'll love it."

But Chase's mind was set. He refused to listen to anyone. Even though some of the roads would probably be closed due to high water, he had to try. He had visualized this moment for too long to change it now.

Chase was strikingly handsome in his three-piece suit and Elizabeth elegantly beautiful in her long, sleek dress, but they did seem a little out of place as they climbed into Chase's dad's pickup truck. Though a car was available, the truck was important to the success of Elizabeth's birthday gift, and Chase hoped not to sway an inch from his original plan.

After dinner at an exquisite Japanese restaurant, Chase ushered Elizabeth back inside the pickup and then placed her birthday gift in her hands. Elizabeth opened the box and inside found what looked like a . . . headband?

"Oh, uh, thanks, Honey," she said, struggling to sound appreciative.

Chase smiled. "You need to wear it over your eyes, like a blindfold."

Intrigued, Elizabeth played along, trying to guess where they were going. At last the truck stopped. Elizabeth heard loud gushing water. "Hmmm. Sounds like we've stopped on a bridge over a rushing river. Is he going to throw me into the water and do away with me?" She laughed nervously as Chase helped her out of the truck. Though it was dry where they stood, she could hear the rain pouring down around them.

"Don't move," Chase said. "I'll be right back."

Elizabeth nodded. He sounded as nervous as she felt! Besides, where did he think she would go? Along with the pelting rain, she suddenly heard music playing. The song was immediately familiar, but she couldn't quite put her finger on why.

Was that the song they had danced to so long ago?

Meanwhile, the doors of the truck opened and closed. She turned toward the noise. "What was he up to?" Finally, she felt Chase return to her side.

"You can take the headband off now," he said, sounding both relieved and out of breath.

It took a moment for Elizabeth's eyes to adjust to the light, but by the headlights of the truck she recognized the old covered bridge, and at the same time remembered the romantic song from a few years before.

Speechless, she looked up at Chase, but he was looking down. Her gaze followed his and she gasped. There was a table with a beautiful tablecloth, a huge bouquet of flowers in a large glass vase, and one chair.

"How did you . . . what's this?"

Chase leaned closer and kissed her, and then pulled the chair out for her. As Elizabeth slowly sat down, he handed her a small white box. On the flooded back country roads of Glass Rock, Ohio, amid century-old buildings, Chase got down on one knee and asked for Elizabeth's heart and her hand in marriage. With trembling lips and eyes full of tears, Elizabeth responded with a resounding, "Yes, yes, yes!"

Commemorating the moment, they engraved their names alongside the names of those who had been there before them, embedding a pledge of their love into the timeworn walls of the picturesque covered bridge. Standing there in the middle of nowhere, with rain beating down all around them, it was as if the old covered bridge covered them in love.

Connie Sturm Cameron

Lucky in Love

My great-granddaughter Samantha slowly turned the pages of an old picture album, then abruptly looked up at me with a question in her eyes. "I've never seen a wedding picture of you, Grandma."

I smiled. It was pleasant sitting beside Samantha, and I suddenly felt the need to share something personal. "That's because none were taken. Not one. Your grandpa and I were the same age as you—nineteen. The young think it's hard starting out these days, and they are right, but it's nothing compared to 1940."

Samantha scooted closer. "Does telling it make you feel sad?"

I shook my head, "No, it was a happy day. At the time, pictures were unimportant; but these many years later, a photo would be nice. I recall the wedding vividly. I'd bought a new dress two days before for one dollar—end-of-the-season clearance—white lace around the bodice and a light-blue street-length skirt. Really beautiful, and appropriate to wear to church later."

Birds singing outside made a musical background, and suddenly I wanted hot chocolate and wondered what forgotten memory from the past had prompted the craving.

"Like a hot chocolate?" I asked. I rose to my feet and headed toward the kitchen before she answered. As I pulled out the ingredients, I continued with my story.

"We were young and optimistic. The Depression appeared to be improving, and we couldn't believe President Roosevelt would let the United States enter an overseas war, but, still, draft rumors spread. We hesitated to marry.

I turned to look at Samantha. "That made Mother uneasy—a young girl should wed soon and not let a good prospect get away!" Samantha smiled and nodded her head in agreement. I stopped for a moment and frowned. "Mother placed pressure on me to set the day, but I decided to keep the chosen date of September fourteenth to myself. Your grandpa needed signed permission from a parent, so both our families were informed on the twelfth, but told it was private."

I stirred the milk in the pan and Samantha got out the glasses and spoons. While I watched her moving about the kitchen, I remembered how different things where when I was nineteen and how badly I had wanted to keep that date a secret, and I laughed out loud.

"Hindsight warns me we should have asked the preacher if he was available."

"The preacher didn't know?" Samantha's voice was laced with disbelief.

I shook my head vehemently. "No! No witness, either. It's hard to imagine two nineteen-year-olds being so uninformed." By now I was laughing so hard, tears ran down my cheeks. I wiped them away and took a sip of hot chocolate.

"We drove the few miles out of town to his house, and guess what? No one was home!" This time Samantha laughed out loud. "So, we sat in the car and waited. We waited and we waited. Finally the family arrived, loaded with groceries. They invited us into their kitchen and there—with borrowed witnesses from next door—we made the famous promise. Until death do us part." A vision of that day filled my mind and I recalled why I had the craving for hot chocolate. Stirring the hot chocolate with the spoon, I said, "I believe we were served sandwiches and hot chocolate."

I exhaled slowly, my mind lingering on the good times that my husband and I have shared since we made the decision to spend our lifetime together.

"Sixty-four years—and we are still together. I'd say it's longer than most modern marriages with their albums of bouquets held close to long flowing dresses, wouldn't you?"

My granddaughter nodded and gave me a hug. "Yes, Grandma, I do."

I hugged her back. "But even so," I said wistfully, "I do wish I had one snapshot." Samantha pulled away and smiled up at me in understanding. It was something in her smile that brought the thought to mind.

"I looked like you, Samantha! When you marry, I'll claim one picture as me!"

Verna L. Simms

Last on the List

I had recorded the marriages of five of my six children in the front of my Bible. By now they had all been married long enough to give me twenty-two grandchildren—all of my children, that is, except for Merna, who had not found the right man. In fact, Merna still lived at home, which filled in the void left by her father when he passed away, but would not be my choice for her in this world, if it were up to me. Each time I glanced at that page in my Bible, my heart would constrict with anguish. Not a day passed that I didn't plead with God to send the right man Merna's way, but days, weeks, months, and years sailed by—and still Merna's life was empty of a mate.

In the past, teaching preschool had seemed to fulfill Merna, but I sensed that it was getting harder and harder for her to have confidence in the future.

One day, she began to weep and confided to me that she was afraid of what would happen to her when I was gone. Who would be there to greet her when she came home from work? How would she manage on her very small salary? I encouraged her as best I could, but my heart ached for her as well, and that night in my bed in the dark I cried, also.

The next day, we talked and she decided she would begin to dream about marriage and the man God had set aside for her. Often after that decision, we looked at wedding magazines and joked and laughed about what someday we believed would happen. Sure she was forty-five years old and there was not a decent, single male in view. That didn't mean that someone wasn't out there—someone as lonely and eager for marriage as she.

One evening, my son-in-law, who lives in Canada, phoned with the news that he had met a very nice single man. The man was a little older than Merna and he had never been married. He was willing to meet Merna if she was willing.

If she was willing! Merna risked rejection and told her brother-in-law that she was game.

A few weeks later, Merna traveled to Canada to meet a certain "Dale Randall." The first date didn't go smoothly; Merna was shy around this sophisticated older man. But the next day, Dale arrived at the door with a beautiful bouquet, and the second date went better.

When she returned home to Idaho, the e-mails began flying back and forth. Soon Dale visited Merna on her own turf. He appreciated her fine qualities and they fell madly in love. Within three months, they were engaged. Suddenly, all of Merna's dreams were coming true.

A week before the wedding, I was sitting in church, and the page with the list of my children and their spouses happened to fall open. The blank line beside Merna's name filled my vision. Quickly, joyfully, and thankfully, I wrote "Dale Randall" on the blank line. When I was finished, I placed the sheet of paper back into the Bible, and knelt down. Bowing my head, I offered my prayers of thanks to God, as I know Merna and Dale already have.

Norma Favor

This Diamond Ring

Once upon a time, more than a century ago, a handsome young man, (who later became my grandfather), got down on one knee and offered a diamond ring to the beautiful young lady who would become my grandmother.

As everyone knows, "A diamond is forever . . . ," so when a man gets on his knee and offers a diamond to a woman, he is offering his heart forever. My grandmother accepted the gift of his heart but not his diamond.

"It's too big," she protested. "I can't wear that."

So he went on a quest for another diamond more to her liking and returned with a smaller one. When the new ring pleased her, he slipped it onto her finger. Then he took the rejected diamond, which was indeed large and brilliant, and had it put into a man's setting and wore it himself, as a token of his love for her.

"Our first son will wear it, too," they decided. But no son arrived.

Their daughter, my mother, received the ring in trust for her first son, but she too had only daughters. Therefore, she resolved to give the ring to her first son-in-law. But when I, her eldest daughter, married, the groom was not my mother's choice, and she doubted the marriage would last, so the beautiful diamond ring remained hidden in its ivory box, deep in the bank vault. Years went by, and for a time the ring and its story was forgotten.

On my twenty-fifth wedding anniversary, my mother withdrew the diamond ring from the vault—where it had rested all of those years—and presented it to my husband.

"Since the marriage has lasted this long, I guess it will survive," she declared. My husband slipped the ring onto his finger and thanked her with a hug, truly grateful to finally be an accepted member of the family.

Later that night, he returned the ring to its small ivory ring box. "It's too big," he said with regret. "I can't wear it."

So now the ring comes out only on very special occasions—weddings, renewals of vows, baptisms, anniversary parties, and, of course, anytime my mother is around. And whenever I see the ring on my husband's finger, I remember seeing that same ring sparkle on my grandfather's strong hand. I wish my husband would wear it more often, but he won't.

"I feel like a Mississippi gambler wearing such fine jewelry," he says each time he carefully returns it to its antique box.

Someday we will pass this special ring on to one of our sons as a token of the love and loyalty that encompasses our family. We have not yet decided which son, but despite this dilemma and despite my mother's early concerns about our marriage lasting, we are all living happily ever after.

Stella Ward Whitlock

Love at First
Suede Coat

As I stepped onto the front porch that day so long ago, a sunny June sky and an explosion of yellow flowers from the golden rain tree in my parent's yard greeted me. I clutched my bridal bouquet tightly and smiled. Then I threw my head back and, squinting into the glorious brightness, thought: "This is a perfect day to marry my best friend!" Soon the whole family, captured by Uncle Frank with his movie camera, was heading to the Church of the Holy Spirit, where friends and relatives waited to celebrate our special day with us.

By today's standards, our wedding would be considered modest—almost tiny. The bridal party consisted of my sister Jean as maid of honor and Clay, my husband's brother-in-law, as best man. Our dear friend Andy acted as official wedding photographer. After the ceremony, my new husband,

Rodger, and I dined at a quaint restaurant with our immediate relatives. From there, the party moved to my mother- and father-in-law's backyard. Under the shade of tall apple trees, guests shared conversation, lemonade, and hugs. Later that night, Rodger and I began our life together with a romantic honeymoon at Strickland's Resort in the cool Pocono Mountains of Pennsylvania.

My mind often drifts back to that warm, wonderful June day, thirty-three years ago. It was a day of new beginnings for me and my husband. Today—three grown children, three grandchildren, and thousands of precious memories later—I realize that it all began with a smile and a very special coat.

For months, I had talked to Rodger on my sister's CB radio, and our friendship had grown. But we hadn't met face-to-face, and I could tell Rodger was as nervous about it as I was. When he stepped through the doorway of my Mother's kitchen, I was immediately drawn to his handsome face. His eyes were the color of early morning skies, and his skin was clear and fair. Wavy, slicked-back blond hair gave him a slight James Dean appearance, and I couldn't take my eyes off him or off his coat! The coat was made of soft, beige suede, with a warm pile lining and knobby, chocolate-colored leather buttons. I wanted to reach out and touch it—and him—but I didn't dare. Smitten with Rodger, and his beautiful coat, I fell in love at first sight.

After a while, Rodger took off his coat and hung it on the back of a kitchen chair. We sat and talked for hours. Over the course of the next few years, he became my steady boyfriend, and my mother's kitchen table became one of our favorite places. It was there that we got to know one another. We laughed, played games, and chatted endlessly. His coat draped across one of the kitchen chairs became a well-known sight.

As is always the case, time did not stand still for us or for our relationship. The Vietnam War loomed on the horizon. Rodger was drafted into the United States Army, and then transferred to Germany. But love cannot be tamped down for long and during one of his rest and recuperation visits, Rodger asked me to become his wife. I accepted without hesitation. Shortly after Rodger returned home safely, we were married.

As our love grew, so did our family. Soon we had three beautiful children—two daughters and one son. Our home was bursting at the seams. To ensure we had some space to ourselves, periodically we went through our belongings, discarding or donating old clothing and toys. But I could never bear to part with my husband's suede coat. For years, it occupied a special place in our hall closet.

Then, while our son, Mike, was a teenager, it became fashionable to wear retro clothing and he began raiding his father's wardrobe. The beloved suede coat now found a home in Mike's closet. Often, I wondered on whose kitchen chair his cologne-scented suede coat might hang, and would it have the same effect on my son's female friends as it once had on me? Mike was every bit as handsome as his dad (minus the James Dean hairdo). But all too soon Mike grew out of the retro phase and the coat found its way back into the hall closet, where it remains.

Today as I look around at my family, I realize there is a new chance for the coat to hang on the back of some lucky young lady's kitchen chair, because now we have two adorable grandsons. Like their Grandpa and Uncle Mike before them, Jake and Eric have sparkling blue eyes and slightly wavy blonde hair. Maybe someday they'll find their way into our hall closet, and the suede coat will once again work its magic.

Susan J. Siersma

A Cut Above

It was more than "Uh-oh," and more than "Oops." It was a full-blown "Oh, no!" and my six-year-old mind was hard-pressed to keep visions of various punishments—each more horrid than the last—from entering my mind. Swallowing hard, I kept my eyes glued to the expression on Mother's face as we both realized what my request had cost her. Our eyes met and held over the string of nearly perfect paper dolls she had just cut from the paper I had handed her.

I had been bored. Mother had been busy. But in the manner of children, I had whined, demanding attention, and Mother, in the way of mothers, had responded.

"Make me some dolls," I pleaded.

"Bring me a piece of paper," Mother answered, without looking up.

Happily, I raced to do her bidding. I have no idea from what drawer or box or closet shelf I extracted the paper, but it was already folded when I handed it to her. Without opening it, she quickly cut it into a garland of dolls. Now, looking at the neat row of paper dolls that hung between us, Mother saw, to her horror, not a line of little girls holding hands—but a legal document stating that Florence Garber and Kenneth White had been united in Holy Matrimony on December 23, 1929. Mother had cut her marriage license into a string of paper dolls!

Knowing full well I was the guilty party, I waited for a reprimand that never came. Instead of giving me the dolls I had requested, Mother told me a story. I'd never heard the story before and haven't forgotten it since.

December 23, 1929, was quite a day: the culmination of a courtship that had begun with a church drama production. In the production, my dad played the role of a blundering suitor who periodically popped up and announced to the character my mother played, "The ring is nearly paid for." By the time the play ended, a mutual affection had developed between them. The rural Iowa of Mother and Daddy's childhood, with its weathered clapboard houses set alongside the corn and the hogs, seemed the ideal setting for romance. Soon Daddy popped the question. I don't know if he played the part of a blundering suitor in real life or not, but I do know Mother said yes.

The wedding would take place in the spacious home of Mother's grandparents. Her grandfather, the local minister, was to perform the ceremony, which was scheduled in the evening.

And so it was. On December 23, 1929, after chores, friends and relatives began to gather . . . but not the groom's parents, who now lived several hundred miles away. The guests mingled as they waited. The hands on the clock moved. Still no groom's parents. The late evening turned to night. The guests remained. The hands on the clock moved. Still: no groom's parents. At about 11:45 P.M. someone suggested they stop the clock to protect the integrity of the legal documents dated December 23.

Finally, at 11:45 P.M., as stated by the irrefutable clock, the groom's parents—detained by farm duties and mud-immersed roads—arrived, and the wedding took place. The vows held, and my parents' love grew over the years, producing quite a string of dolls: seven children, twenty-some grandchildren, and scads of great- and great-great-grandchildren.

Mother ended her story and looked down at the paper dolls in her hand. A slow smile came to her lips. Turning her marriage license into a string of dolls had in no way diminished her marriage.

"Since then, we have never been apart for an anniversary," she said softly. "And we never will."

In December 2000 Mother and Daddy celebrated their anniversary together, as they had done for seventy-one years. Early in 2001, Daddy died. Later that same year Mother became ill and passed away in December, just before their anniversary. The tradition holds: They have never been apart for an anniversary. And they never will. But if, someday, in the ages to come, some little seraph hands Mother a folded piece of paper and requests paper dolls, I'm guessing this time around Mother will take a good look at the paper in her hands before she starts cutting.

Roberta Rhodes

Unwilling Accomplice

On the day our brother Leslie was to be married, our already married sister Shirley returned to our family home in Beech Creek, Pennsylvania, with a devious plan in mind. She went into the barn, scooped up a measure of wheat, and brought it into the house. Nodding for me to follow, she headed up the stairs to the bridal suite our mother had prepared for Leslie and his new wife. With a few deft moves, she stripped the bed of its linens. I watched, slack-jawed, as she spread the wheat over the mattress. Together, we remade the bed. Shirley said her goodbyes and drove away, leaving me behind, a puzzled eleven-year-old wondering about her strange behavior.

Eight years later, in 1954, my sister Roberta, my best friend and confidante, set her wedding date at a time I could be home from my college studies in Tennessee. We were a close-knit family of nine, and she wanted us sisters to be her attendants. Roberta lived with our widowed Aunt Velma in Mill Hall, so the day before the wedding, Shirley came back to the farm, picked me up, and took me to visit our aunt. After exchanging pleasantries, my sister excused herself and went upstairs.

In a few minutes, Shirley called to me. Obedient little sister that I was, I mounted the stairs to see what she wanted. She met me at the head of the stairwell and indicated I should follow her into Roberta's bedroom.

I hesitated. We kids had been taught at an early age to respect each other's privacy and not to invade one another's space. I stepped into the room with misgivings, wondering what she had in mind.

Shirley glanced around, obviously looking for something. When she saw my sister's suitcase—already packed for her honeymoon—she picked it up, set it on the bed, and began to lift out the garments.

My heart raced. This was a violation of Roberta's privacy, and I didn't think we ought to be in her room when she wasn't there. We certainly should not have been pawing through her clothing! When the suitcase was nearly empty, Shirley smiled and held up my sister's wedding negligee as though it were a trophy. She laid it on the bed and whipped a needle and thread out of her pocket.

I gaped at her as she picked up the lovely gown and began to stitch the bottom together. Back and forth her needle flew until she had used up the long thread. I had learned how to short sheet a bed in college and this deed immediately reminded me of that prank. When she was finished, Shirley put her needle away and put the clothing back into the suitcase. Then we went back downstairs, and shortly thereafter she took me home.

The newlyweds left for their honeymoon after the wedding festivities, and I returned to college with a bit of guilt about the incident and the fact that I had unwillingly been an accomplice. Roberta was my best friend and I felt I owed her an apology. The opportunity came the next summer when I was home from school and Roberta invited me to her house to look at wedding photos. As we relived that happy occasion, my conscience got the best of me.

Swallowing hard, I declared, "I have a confession to make." Then I poured out the entire sordid story of what I had inadvertently helped Shirley do on the night before her wedding.

Roberta looked into my unhappy eyes for what seemed like hours. I couldn't tell if she was trying to compose herself or come up with a response to my disloyalty. Then her eyes lit up, she threw back her head, and she laughed wildly. "Don't worry, Hope," she said, apparently deciding I was old enough to learn one of the more scandalous aspects of married life. "I didn't discover my gown had been sewed shut until last month when Richard and I spent the night with some friends."

When Arthur and I were married a few years later, I have a hunch Shirley had another prank in mind. Unfortunately for her, she didn't get to carry it out because we spent our wedding night in a motel.

Hope Irvin Marston

Riding into the Sunset

The summer I was fourteen years old, I was in love with my horse. Late one afternoon, after two long trail rides, I crawled up into the hayloft at the stables where I boarded him to rest a bit. I was afraid I might startle anyone coming up for hay, so I lay directly in front of the ladder. I dozed in the late afternoon sun, until I felt a rock hit my back.

Raising my head and looking around the loft, I peered into the dark corners but saw nothing. I put my head back down. That's when I felt a second rock hit my shoulder. I raised my head again and looked down. That's when I saw him.

I recognized him as the boy who had a horse in the stall next to mine. He was wearing blue jeans and cowboy boots. Normally he looked out of place at the horse stables, dressed in slacks, shirt, and a wide tie. He was smiling. No words passed between us, just a look, a glare, a smart-aleck grin. I put my head back down, assuming that he would stop throwing rocks now that he knew someone was in the loft. That's when the third rock hit me.

Raising my head again, I glared at him. "Go away and leave me alone," I said in as threatening a tone as I could manage. He just continued to smile at me, saying nothing. Then he left.

A few days later, I saw him again.

"You know," I confronted him, "you oughta feed that nag a little more often. He tried to bite me the other day when I fed my horse."

He smiled again. Then he asked, "You wanna go to the movies with me Saturday night?"

That was a surprise. "I don't know," I replied, wondering if he even knew my name. "I've been invited to go to a party with one boy but another one asked me to go to the rodeo with him. I haven't decided what I'm gonna do yet," I smiled back, pleased to let him know that he was not the only boy around who was interested in me.

"You think that's cute, don't you?" he said, still smiling.

I glared back, angry at his challenge.

"You really think that you can tell me you're goin' out with some other guy and I'll just say, 'Oh, that's okay.' You expect me to kiss you right here and now, don't you, and tell you that it doesn't matter, I'll be waiting for you when you get back."

Well, that might be nice, I thought. "I most certainly do not!" I lied, turning to walk past him. I did not like him reading me so easily.

And that's when he did exactly what he had said he would do. Reaching out as I tried to push past him, he took me by the shoulders, turned me around, kissed me, and said, "You go ahead and do whatever you want. I'll be waiting when you get back."

And I did. I went to the rodeo. I sat there in the rodeo stands, staring up at the moon and ignoring my date, wondering about that boy at the horse stables and what he really wanted from me.

I started asking around the stables about him. He was nineteen years old, five years older than I, and worked full-time as a relief manager for a chain of local department stores—that's why he wore slacks and a tie when he came out to feed his horse. He also went to college part-time and drove a metallic blue Mustang.

It wasn't long before we were seeing quite a lot of each other, mostly at the stables with our horses, but sometimes riding out into the country to the little house he rented with his brothers. I found out he had noticed me long before I had noticed him.

"See that girl over there," he had told one of his friends before our meeting. "I'm gonna marry her."

"You're crazy, Mike. She's jailbait," his friend replied, referring to my young age.

But that didn't stop him. He pursued me anyway. As my parents became aware of how serious our relationship was, they started restricting the amount of time we could spend together. I offered to run away from home and live with him somewhere out of state. He refused.

"I want you as my wife for the rest of my life, or I don't want you at all," was his reply. By the time I was fifteen and he was twenty, he had finished two years of college and we decided we had waited long enough. We drove his Mustang across the border and were married. We celebrated with lunch in the Cadillac Bar and bought an alabaster chess set as a wedding gift.

That was thirty-four years ago. It's been a long journey, but no more difficult than for other couples who married later in life than we did.

Recently, we were lying in bed watching TV. During a commercial break, he told me he felt guilty for marrying me when I was so young.

"I stole your youth," he lamented.

I hit the remote and changed channels. "Then why'd you do it?" I asked him. I hit the remote again.

"Because I was afraid if I didn't marry you, someone else would," he answered.

"Might have," I replied honestly.

He propped himself up on one arm and looked at me. "You know something? I'm not sorry. I'm not sorry at all."

I turned toward him. "You know something? Neither am I."

After he kissed me for a long time, we muted the volume and held each other in the blue glow of the TV screen.

Sally Clark

One Day in the Gulf of Georgia

I leaned over the ladder in Suzanne's swimming pool so that I would be sure to catch the swimmer's ear when she surfaced. I had been instantly smitten by her beauty and grace in the pool—an Esther Williams crush, so to speak. Her name was Kay. She was a friend of Suzanne's, my date for tonight's Mr. Touchdown Dance.

Droplets of water scattered like gems as she tossed her hair from side to side in the reflected light. She patted her face with a terrycloth towel, and I introduced myself. Then, perhaps overly hasty and anxious, I leapt from quick introduction to asking her to the movie the following Friday. In words that poured over me like hot wax, she promptly informed me that she was going steady. It was 1959—a time when the words "going steady" were respected covenants akin to those other oaths, like "King's X," and "cross my heart and hope to die." And die I did. In an instant, my hopes were dashed. Maybe I shouldn't have rushed things so.

"I'm going with Jimmy Pollock," she said. "You know him, he drives a Buick. He's also in DeMolay."

"Jimmy Pot-luck," I mumbled mockingly, well out of earshot range.

The bar was thus set fairly high. For sure, Buicks and DeMolay were daunting credentials to overcome. I was just a Chevy guy and not a member of anything.

Six months passed before I saw her again. I was at Neely's, a drive-in barbecue eatery and high school hangout. There she was, in the back seat of a convertible full of squealing girls.

"Hi again," I said, trying to mimic the little lip-curl that Elvis was so adored for. "How is old Jimmy Pollock these days? I haven't seen him around."

"Oh. You didn't hear? His daddy sent him to military school in Arizona. Maybe he'll come back for the summer, but who knows?"

Her words were like happy-grams from Western Union. Once again, the anticipation of a date spurred a hasty tongue. My next words must be bold, I thought. I walked over to the convertible and without hesitation, asked if I could call her. This time, a smile rewarded my forwardness. She handed me her phone number—penned in lipstick on a

Neely's napkin. It was all the stuff of a James Dean movie.

After the Neely's reunion we dated like a train schedule. Every weekend was reserved, every spare moment claimed. The intensity soon caught the eye of Kay's parents, and diplomatic relations began to strain. Her father's handshakes became wincingly firm when he greeted me at the door. Her mother transfixed on my face with increasing scrutiny, hoping I might vaporize under her supernova glare. Kay and I were no longer left alone when I visited, and there was always a pair of beady eyes straining over the raised newspaper her father held as a decoy. In a lesson most parents fail to learn, such imposed exile serves only to make the absent heart grow fonder. The first week after graduation, in a bold and calculated move, we eloped.

Donaldsonville was a small town in southwest Georgia, just across the Chattahoochee River from Florida. Though Donaldsonville sought fame for its strawberry fields, it had caught my attention for its reputation as a marriage mill to serve the under-aged. Though too young to marry under Florida law, Georgia welcomed such love-desperados as us. At the courthouse, a simple license application was completed and we were sent to obtain blood tests. Like a low-budget version of the prolific neon lights that abound in Las Vegas, Donaldsonville hyped

"Marriage Blood Tests!" on every Dr Pepper sign, at every service station in town.

The Colquitt Street Gulf station banner read: "Marriage Tests While U Wait," a slogan that seemed expedient for our needs. We gave blood and waited on the results, persevering through a Studebaker lube job and a siren-blaring wrecker call. It was a tense time, but soon a man wearing the embroidered name "Sonny" came forward with a reassuring verdict.

"Y'all's blood's fine," he said. I half expected him to show me a dipstick for proof. Instead, he scrawled our blood types on a garage repair receipt and said to return it to the courthouse. I couldn't help but notice that our $10 fee amounted to three times the cost of the Studebaker lube. Although I never saw the backroom lab, I dismissed the high cost as necessary to ensure that his expensive medical equipment remained in absolute sanitary condition.

At the courthouse, the clerk recorded our blood tests and we were ushered in to the "Ordinary," who was introduced as "Her Honor Mary." This court official turned out to be something of a cross between a justice and an auctioneer. The ceremony was a staccato of rapid-fire whereases and therefores. Her Honor eventually paused at the only familiar words in the litany, "If these are the wishes of the betrothed, say I do."

We did.

"You are hereby lawfully united as man and wife," she concluded.

Pleased, Kay and I turned toward one another. But before I could kiss my bride and legitimize the whirlwind vows, I was interrupted. The Ordinary presented us with a marriage gift box adorned with a white ribbon. Inside were sample-size cosmetics, non prescription ointments and creams, Midol, and a ladies' shower cap. On the cap were stenciled the words, "McAdoo Insurance—we keep you dry in the wet spots of life."

The finality of marriage quickly calmed the stormy relationship with Kay's parents, and the birth of their first grandson two years later elevated me to hero status.

Now, forty-plus years later, I still hold a fondness for that little Georgia town, Colquitt's Gulf Station, and the cattle-call marriage mill at the courthouse. And while nothing about that day was Buick—certainly not DeMolay—I still hold the winner's prize.

Lad Moore

Let It Rest

My wife, Penney, and I were returning from an outing to the Antler's Bar and Grill in Sault Ste. Marie, Michigan, where all the animals are stuffed and those that aren't are stewed. That's as close as I wanted to get to nature and wildlife on a bitter winter night. But, wouldn't you know it, on the road home the car stuttered, yammered, and then stalled next to a snowbank on the shoulder of the road.

Now what?

Penney simply stared straight ahead as if waiting for me to tear open the hood and fiddle and squeeze and poke till the only thing I had going was a bad case of the chilblains. And I just knew that when I got back in the car she would calmly say, "Why don't we just let it rest." But not this time. I wasn't going to give her the satisfaction.

She always says that. When the toaster doesn't toast—let it rest. When the garbage disposal seizes up—let it rest. Penney doesn't know anything about thermal relays and reset buttons, but every time I start to tell her about those things, she smiles like a mountaintop guru with the answer to life: Let it rest. And, of course, she's right part of the time, but she doesn't know why (and couldn't care less). All I know is that we have a whole corner of the basement filled with appliances resting. Some of them have been resting for twenty years or more.

It was during our honeymoon when I first discovered my wife's penchant for patience and heard the first chord in the symphony of our life together. During a long stroll through the Charleston historic district, we happened upon a pre–Civil War cemetery. Penney noticed the headstones with R.I.P. carved across the top.

"I wonder what that means?" she asked.

"Rest in peace," I replied.

A slow smile of recognition spread across her face. Other people, in other times, knew her refrain.

"Well," I declared. "Don't plan on putting anything like that on my grave marker. I'm not happy to sit still. I never will be. I plan to be turning over in my grave on a regular basis."

"Yes, dear," she replied.

Being a young newlywed, I felt I owed her a more thorough explanation. I added, "I like to get right at a thing. For example, if I catch a cold, I want to smother that virus with antihistamines and night syrups and day fizzies and tons of water and bowls of soup and steaming baths and full-body sweats."

"Yes, dear," she replied.

Not completely convinced she understood where I was coming from, I told her a story. "There was a man stuck behind a delivery truck while driving down a narrow country road. Every couple of miles the truck would stop. The driver would get out and run around the truck and bang it on the sides with a stick. The man in the car was getting exasperated. Finally, when they got to the next town, he pulled up next to the truck driver and demanded an explanation. 'I'm sorry,' the truck driver apologized. 'You see, mister, I'm carrying 10,000 pounds of canaries on a 5,000 pound load-limit road and I have to keep half of them birds flying all the time.'

"That's me," I announced. "I'm like that truck driver. I like to keep things moving."

"Yes, dear" was all she said.

Well, I'm older now and have mellowed some. I no longer insist on my way being the only way. I've learned a few things from her. Maybe it's all the gardening she does. There's a rhythm to it all: a time for planning, a time for planting, a time for growing, and a time for harvesting. Then she cans the vegetables and fruit and lines them on a shelf where, of course, they wait. Or maybe she gets her outlook from having babies. You can't rush babies. It's a long ride, so you might as well relax. She has taken a lot of trips.

These days, if I come home from work all strung out over my boss, my wife counsels patience. If I watch the news and get flustered by the happenings around the globe, my wife thinks it will all work out in good time. When my daughter brings a baritone-voiced, gangly lad into our home and I want to hand-wrestle him, my wife serenely ushers him out the door saying, "I'm sure my husband will be all right as soon as he rests for a while."

So maybe after all of these years of marriage, I can admit that she is right. This night, in this snowdrift, I'm going to let it rest. That having been decided, I sat back and looked straight ahead.

Penney looked over at me. Concern laced her voice when she asked, "Well, aren't you going to do something? You know, like look under the hood, jump the carburetor, or goose the battery or whatever it is that you do?"

"No," I replied in a level voice. "I thought I would just let it rest for a while."

"Are you nuts?" she screamed. "We could freeze to death out here!"

Suddenly she jumped from the vehicle and began walking back the way we had come. With a satisfied grin, I watched for a moment, and then I opened the car door and joined her.

Joseph K. Novara

Blue Velvet Dress

Fontaine was nervous about meeting her blind date. She had been surprised enough when Joan, one of her high school students, asked if she would be interested in meeting her Uncle Robert. At first, Fontaine wasn't sure if she should go out with Joan's uncle. But she was new to the Florida coast; surely it wouldn't hurt to meet and mingle with more people her own age. Besides, she was bored. Her weekends consisted of grading papers, washing her hair, and watching television. Though she'd met some young men through her roommate, nothing had clicked. She needed a night out, and the idea of going on a blind date was appealing.

While Fontaine curled her hair, she worried that she and Robert would have nothing in common. She hadn't even asked Joan what Robert looked like or what his interests were. All she knew was that he worked for a family air-conditioning company and that the family was originally from New York. Fontaine was also worried about her own appearance. At five feet six inches, she was taller than many women, and she had a larger than average Greek nose. To top it all off, she was an English teacher, and some men seemed to be quite intimidated by a career-driven woman. She hoped that wouldn't be the case with Robert.

When the knock came, Fontaine felt a flutter. She opened the door and looked out. There stood a short, dark-haired, handsome man with bright blue eyes. He looked up at her and smiled warmly. The dimples in his cheeks stirred the butterflies in Fontaine's stomach, and for the first time in her life, she felt speechless. She loved dimples, and his were absolutely perfect.

"How are ya?" he asked, sounding like a New Yorker. "I'm Robert," he added, his smile sincere. "Joan told me about you. Would you like to go to this restaurant around the corner? Then I'd like to take you to one of my favorite bars for an after-dinner drink."

Fontaine didn't drink often, but she wanted to get to know Robert better. Wherever he wanted to take her was fine.

"Sure. So . . . Joan told you all about me?"

Robert shook his head. "Not exactly. She did tell me that you were one tough teacher, though."

Fontaine smiled. "Maybe she hoped that fixing me up would take my mind off her papers."

Robert chuckled—his laugher infectious—and before long they were chatting like they'd known one another for years. Dinner conversation went smoothly, too, especially when the topic moved to music. Robert became animated when he talked about his large record collection. Fontaine was impressed that he enjoyed the same kind of music that she did. Before dinner was over, she and Robert had talked about everything from records to religion.

Aside from being a few inches shorter than she was, Robert seemed to be the perfect man. And while his height wasn't an issue with her, Fontaine knew it might bother him. If it did, she knew he'd never ask her out again and she could already feel herself falling for him.

As they entered the small nightclub that evening, it seemed everyone knew Robert. Fontaine's heart fell. Robert must visit the nightclub often. Did that mean he had lots of lady friends? She decided to make the best of this evening, at least, and pretended the idea of him dating other women didn't bother her.

Robert led her to a table near a large black piano and pulled out a chair for her. The baby grand was placed in the corner, near a window that overlooked the ocean. It was a very beautiful and romantic setting.

"Oh, wonderful!" Fontaine exclaimed. "I love listening to piano music! Who's playing?"

"What kind of tunes do you like?" Robert asked. "I'll make a request." When Fontaine hesitated, he asked, "What about 'Fly Me to the Moon,' 'Alley Cat,' or 'Blue Velvet'? "

"Oh, 'Blue Velvet'," Fontaine said. "I love that song."

Robert nodded. With a smile on his face, he walked toward the piano. While Fontaine watched in surprise, he sat down on the bench, put his hands on the keys, and began to play "Blue Velvet."

As Fontaine listened to Robert sing her that romantic song, her heart melted.

On the way home that evening, Robert stopped at a grocery store to pick up some soda. Instead of waiting in the car, Fontaine went in with him. Every second with him seemed dreamy, and she didn't want it to end.

When they crossed into the frozen food section, a young boy looked up and pointed at Fontaine. "Look, Mommy, that mommy is bigger than that daddy!"

As the mother whisked her child away with a hurried, "Sorry," a blush spread across Fontaine's cheeks. She had completely forgotten that she was taller than Robert. All she knew was that Robert was a sweet man and she enjoyed being with him.

"Love comes in all sizes," Robert announced to the retreating mother and boy.

Fontaine's blush deepened, but inside all she could think about was that she hoped he would call again. But as one week grew into two, she felt sure there would be no second date.

When Robert finally called, the phone never stopped ringing.

They joined a church, got married, and had two children. They even sang in the church choir together. When it came to their relationship, there were no height restrictions. Robert and Fontaine listened to their hearts, not their eyes.

On their tenth wedding anniversary, to commemorate a very special blind date, Fontaine wore a beautiful blue velvet dress that matched Robert's eyes to perfection. And as I watched my parents that evening, they gazed into one another's eyes as if they had been transported back in time to a place where nothing mattered except a piano, a beautiful moonlit night, and a young couple on a new adventure.

Fontaine Wallace, as told to Michele
Wallace Campanelli

An Ancient Treasure

In the corner of my bedroom sits an item that I have never liked, even though I recognize it as a priceless treasure. It is the heavy, solid-oak rocking chair that belonged, in reverse order, to my father, my grandmother, and my great-grandmother.

Despite the fact that the rocking chair is the only piece of antique furniture I own, I'm honor-bound to keep it—Daddy gave it to me as part of my wedding gift way back in the summer of 1950. On occasions when I have tripped over one of the heavy, protruding rockers, I have calmed myself by recalling the story Daddy lovingly told when he gave me the chair.

My great-grandparents, Caroline and Robert, married in South Carolina in 1837 but soon migrated to Alabama where they acquired farmland and raised a large family. Caroline often rocked her children in her rocking chair, thereby catching a few minutes of rest for herself.

One day Robert came home with a team of oxen and a covered wagon. He'd heard news of good land available for homesteading in Louisiana and had already sold the family farm. Planning for the long trip west began immediately. His one stipulation to Caroline was that nonessential items must be left behind, for they would need to travel light. Like an obedient wife, Caroline packed their clothes into trunks, made bedrolls, tied the kitchen necessities on the outside of the wagon, and loaded the food supplies on a pack mule. Then, with fire in her eyes, she announced that she and the older children would walk because under no circumstances would she leave her heavy rocking chair behind.

When their sons returned from fighting for the Confederate States Army, the family packed the wagon again. This time they headed for Texas. Robert died along the way, but Caroline and her children brought the team and wagon—and the rocking chair—safely to Comanche County in Texas, where they took advantage of the fertile land and enjoyed a good source of year-round water.

Times were hard when my grandmother, Nancy Jane, Caroline's twelfth and final child, married my grandfather, James, in 1877. The only dowry her mother had to offer Nancy Jane was a well-filled hope chest, one milk cow, two hogs, and the old oak rocking chair. In her old age, Caroline went to live with Nancy Jane and James, and rocked all of her grandchildren in that chair, including my father, Alex.

In the course of his story, Daddy shed not a tear until he reached the part where his mother gave him the old family rocking chair at the time of his marriage to Mother in 1913. Daddy said he was now passing the chair on to me, the youngest child and the last to marry. He hoped I appreciated the pretty velvet-covered cushions Mother had made for the backrest and seat.

As Daddy dried his tears, a memory from my childhood surfaced. Once again, I could hear Mother's voice singing hymns while she rocked me to sleep, and I suddenly understood Daddy's tears.

World War I, the Great Depression, and World War II displaced and disrupted my parents' lives in many ways. They moved often, always seeking a place that offered a better, more profitable way of life and good opportunities for their children. The rocker moved with them every time. Over the years, it required frequent repairs, but Daddy was determined to keep it operational, for it had a destiny: Someday it would belong to one of his own children.

Today, as I remember that long-ago conversation with my father, I see the rocking chair with new eyes, and it takes on a different appearance. How blessed I am to own it. It is a beautiful and treasured heirloom that survived heavy usage by many people and traveled countless miles before it reached my home. Someday I will proudly pass it on to one of my children or grandchildren on his or her wedding day, and tears will come to my eyes when I get to the part where my father passed it on to me.

Pat Capps Mehaffey

Falling in Love

Pine trees shaded the small group of family and friends gathered in the mountains of Wrightwood, California, that August day. Committing to each other our love and our future, Dan slipped the ring on my finger. In thirty years it has not been off.

The words we engraved in our wedding bands were plucked from an old Fleetwood Mac song about owning and inventing the future you want. That vision served us well over the years as we created a life, a family, and a future together.

Knowing that a good marriage is harder than it looks, we invested in supporting each other's dreams. Knowing that love needs nurturing to grow and prosper, we made our relationship a priority. Knowing that mind reading was not a skill either of us had, we put honest communication as a central part of our life.

Over the years, we felt we did a pretty good job creating the future we wanted to face: good family, good jobs, good health, and good marriage. We were best friends spending as much time as possible together. With each passing year, we fell more in love. And so it went for our first twenty-five years.

Maybe it was the stress of parents' deaths, increased demands at work, challenges of building a house, stock market tumbles, or an outbreak of menopause. Maybe it was all those things. Maybe it was none of them. Whatever it was, gradually our words became peppered with an edge, our disagreements a little more frequent, our hand-holding to fall asleep a little less predictable. Each change insignificant, a single drop of water. But, the drops blended into a drizzle, and in time hints of erosion appeared.

It was not an easy trip. Together in the car for five days moving from Paoli, Pennsylvania, to Whitefish, Montana, the fuse between us was short. We knew things were not right. Yet our escalating tensions persisted as we each held tightly to harbored grievances. Dan suggested detouring to where we went to graduate school. As we walked the campus, visited old haunts, and relived memories of falling in love, we remembered why we fell in love with each other in the first place. Reconnecting to that love, we fell in love again.

What eroded in those life-altering shifts was not our love. What eroded was our focus on continuing to invent the everyday future we wanted to face. I've learned that even a few drops of miscommunication, disappointment, or hurt can grow to significance if unattended. So, as the quote in our wedding rings takes on new meaning, I wish my husband and best friend a very happy thirtieth anniversary. May we continue to fall in love with each other forever.

Nan Schindler Russell

Memories in the Making

In my role as father of the bride, I had great plans for my daughter's stroll down the aisle. All seemed to be going according to plan until I entered the cathedral and got my first peek at the most beautiful bride I had seen in thirty-nine years. My little girl was just as beautiful as her mother had been on our special day.

She was my shimmering princess, dressed in the lovely wedding gown that she and her mother had kept hidden from me. In that instant, all of my clever fatherly counsel tangled with my nervously bobbing Adam's apple. Not a single wise utterance escaped my choking throat.

"Hello, beautiful," I managed, completely undone by her radiance.

Karen smiled and gently placed her arm in mine. Taking a deep breath, we began her wedding march down a seemingly mile-long aisle, salty trickles making their way down my face with each step.

Following the ceremony, I danced with my daughter at the nearby country inn. As we stepped onto the dance floor, I hesitated as the song "Wind Beneath My Wings" began. The touching line about discovering you are someone's hero, sung to me by my daughter, was nearly my downfall. My tear ducts hadn't worked this hard since her mother and I were wed so long ago.

Eventually, I surrendered my now married daughter to her mother and withdrew to a quiet corner. As I watched them dance, I looked from one beautiful face to the other and a different day came to mind. My hair was longer and less gray, but on that day I danced with the very same beautiful woman my daughter now danced with, her mother—my bride—Joan. As I watched them that day, a trembling smile formed on my lips, and I hoped with all of my heart that Karen and her new husband would find at least half of the happiness that Joan and I have found on our journey together, for even half would be more than enough to carry them on their new journey as man and wife.

Walter McElligott

A Love to Last

like girls?—me? Gee, I was just a Missouri farm boy. I didn't know much about girls. Feeding chickens, gathering eggs, milking cows, slopping the hogs?—that's what I knew about. I was also busy being the oldest of three boys. My brothers were always in fights or doing something foolish. I had to look out for them. No time for girls.

One Sunday morning in 1937, about the time I was in the eighth grade, Mom shined up her three "stair-step" boys and took us to Faucett Baptist Church. The church was without a pastor, but an out-of-town preacher visited that Sunday, so they asked him to preach.

Now I'm sure he was a fine preacher, but the one I really had my eye on was his daughter. She was the prettiest girl I ever saw. I just couldn't take my eyes off her. When we stood to sing, she glanced my way.

I think she saw me looking at her. As we sat down, she peeked at me again and smiled a little. I turned beet red.

Most Sundays, my wiggly brothers distracted me, but that Sunday, she was the distraction. I gazed at her soft brown hair and slight smile, entranced by her every move. After church, my mom walked over to speak to the preacher's wife. I went right along with her to get a close-up look at this new girl. We were both too shy to speak, but I wondered if her heart might be pounding just like mine.

I watched as she helped her dad put on his over-coat. I thought to myself, *she can help me like that any day.* When we got home, I told my mom, "I'm going to marry that girl some day."

She laughed. "Why, Wayne Watkins, you'll meet a lot of girls before that time comes."

After a year of not seeing the girl of my dreams, our church called that visiting preacher to be our pastor. Just think of it––Norma Deane Schudle would be moving here to Faucett, Missouri, and we would be going to the same high school and church.

We both played violin in the high school orchestra. Her mother asked us to play our violins for church, which, fortunately, required practices at her house—lots of practices. It grew to be a habit that whenever my mom and dad rode into town, they dropped me off at her house. I visited with her or "practiced " until I heard the squeaky brakes of Mom and Dad's old '28 Chevy.

After high school graduation, we both attended a business school twelve miles away in St. Joseph, Missouri. I traded a cow for partial payment of my tuition. I was too poor to afford a car, so I rode my bicycle two and a half miles to Norma's house and paid a friend a dollar a week to drive us from there to St. Joseph. I sure was sweet on that girl. My love for her grew deeper every day, and somewhere along the way, she grew to love me back.

At age eighteen, I applied for a Civil Service job and received a telegram telling me to report to Washington, D.C., as a clerk-typist making a whopping $1,440 per year. Imagine this old farm boy getting on a Greyhound bus and going to the big city of Washington. I had to buy a suitcase because I had never traveled so far.

I sure missed Norma. We had planned that after I worked five months, I would return home so we could get married. I wrote to Norma's parents asking for their blessing and reminded them that I could easily support her.

With the Depression and war going on, we could not afford a big wedding. On June 20, 1942, family members attended our simple home ceremony, with Norma's father officiating. I gave her a rose corsage to wear on her lacy blue dress. One of my brothers and a neighbor girl stood up with us as best man and maid of honor.

Our "honeymoon" consisted of one night in a hotel in St. Joseph for $3. Norma's Aunt Myrtle drove us there. As a little joke, Aunt Myrtle tied Norma's pajama legs and arms in knots.

The next day we rode the bus back to Faucett to say our goodbyes to our families and friends. As we boarded another bus for Washington, my parents threw rice on us. We found a two-room apartment and had to share a bathroom with others down the hall. It was small, but we were so in love that we didn't notice. We rode the streetcar together to our jobs in the morning and back home in the evening.

After a short six months, I received my draft notice and was inducted into the army. Heartbroken, Norma returned home to stay with her parents while I went overseas. Now I was truly a long way from home. I had never dated any other girl but my one true love, and here we were, separated a whole world apart. I anxiously awaited her letters and wrote when I could.

Nine months later, I received a long-awaited cablegram—*Daughter born all well and safe.*

I sent back: *Received cablegram happiest man in world glad you are well love you as always Wayne Watkins.*

It wasn't until eighteen months later that I was able to return to my wife. We clung to each other, hardly able to believe that we were together again. Then I looked down to see, for the first time, my eighteen-month-old daughter toddling into the room. What a happy reunion.

Wayne Watkins, as told to Joyce Cordell

Contributors

Nancy Baker ("Come, Grow Old with Me") resides in College Station, Texas, with her husband of forty-five years. After retirement from Texas A&M University, she pursued her lifelong love of writing and has been published in national magazines and anthologies. She directs the ministry to the sick program at her church and is a hospice volunteer.

Rachel Beanland ("Faithful Pie") is a writer who, like her father, does believe in love at first sight. She is a member of the South Carolina Writers Workshop and lives in Columbia, South Carolina, with her husband, Kevin, whom, coincidentally, she met and fell in love with all in the same evening.

Nancy J. Bennett ("Going to the Fireworks") lives and writes on Vancouver Island. Her work can also be seen in various inspirational anthologies, including *A Cup of Comfort for Sisters*, and in magazines like *Young Rider*, *Lake Country Journal*, *Presbyterian Today*, *The Christian Science Monitor*, *The Anglican Journal*, *Woman of Spirit*, *Glad Tidings*, and *Messenger of the Sacred Heart*. She raises very small chickens and reads them recipes when they are lax in their laying.

Ed Boyd ("Sunny Tomorrows") is a retired psychologist studying journalism at the Cambridge Center for Adult Education. He has studied with Jane Katims for four years.

Barbara Brady ("The Wedding Ring"), a retired registered nurse, lives in Topeka, Kansas, with her husband of almost fifty years. She enjoys church, sunflowers, books, volunteer activities, and—most of all—her family and friends. Barbara is the author of *A Variety of Gifts*, *Smiling at the Future*, and *Seasoned with Salt*. Her work has been published in various markets.

Stephanie Ray Brown ("My Prince Charming Wore Roller Skates") happily tumbles through life with her husband, Terry, and their two children, Savannah, nine, and Cameron, six. This stay-at-home-mother and midnight writer (she writes when she has tucked everyone in bed) has been blessed to be included in several anthologies. Stephanie is tickled every time a story so near and dear to her heart touches other people's hearts, too.

Terry Burns ("Grandpa Doesn't Eat Carrots") has a new *Circuit Rider* series beginning with *Mysterious Ways*, which gives him seventeen books in print. His trade paperback *To Keep a Promise* was a finalist for the Eppie award (e-book form), and was nominated for the Willa Award. *Don't I Know You?* and *Trails of the Dime Novel* are also available. His works can be found at *www.terryburns.net*.

Connie Sturm Cameron ("The Covered Bridge") is a freelance writer residing in Glenford, Ohio, with her husband, Chuck. Their children, Chase and Chelsea, are both in college. Connie has been published in dozens of periodicals and is the author of the book *God's Gentle Nudges*.

Michele Wallace Campanelli ("Blue Velvet Dress") is a national bestselling author. Her work has been published in various anthologies and she has penned many novels, including *Keeper of the Shroud* and *Margarita*.

Suzanne Cherry ("A Lasting Affair") is an associate professor of English and the director of the Swamp Fox Writing Project. Outside class, she spends most of her time reading, writing, and enjoying small-town life in South Carolina.

Michelle Ciarlo-Hayes ("Flying to the Altar") lives in Elkins Park, Pennsylvania, with her husband, Marty, their son, Daniel, and two lovable mutts. Originally from Virginia, Michelle earned her B.A. in English at Mary Washington College and later completed her M.S. in Women's Studies at the University of Oxford, England. She now enjoys being a mom, teaching yoga, and writing . . . when she can find a few moments to herself, that is!

Nan B. Clark ("Embedded Bliss") is a writer and artist whose husband, Tom, has loyally supported her work even when it cluttered up the house.

Sally Clark ("Riding into the Sunset") lives happily with her husband, Mike, in Fredericksburg, Texas, where she writes and publishes poetry, children's stories, and greeting cards. Although they do not have horses anymore, they do have a ranch at the edge of town where they love to sit on the hill and watch the sunset.

Sharon Love Cook ("Miracle or Coincidence?") has had her work appear in various publications, including several anthologies. Sharon is an active member of the Mystery Writers of America and has an M.F.A. in writing.

Joyce Cordell ("A Love to Last") is a former music teacher. She now writes devotionals, Bible studies, and screenplays. Her dad, Wayne Watkins, wrote some wonderful slices of early Americana in an eighteen-page notebook. He presented it to Joyce on her birthday in May before he died in October 1999. Joyce took his and her mother's words and combined them with her own to form the true story she shares with us today.

Darcy Crowder ("Taking the Plunge") is an aspiring romance novelist, currently at work on her first manuscript. She is a member of Romance Writers of America, Georgia Romance Writers, and a board member of a small local writer's group, Mainstreet Writers Association. She has been happily married to the man of her dreams for twenty years and has, indeed, put down roots and raised a family.

Jean Davidson ("The Trousseau"), former administrative assistant, took early retirement several years ago and is now a full-time student at Idaho State University in Pocatello, Idaho. She enjoys studying whatever piques her interest and claims her greatest passions are being with her family and writing their stories.

Bob Davis ("Asking Dad") spent thirty years as a historian for the U.S. Air Force, retiring in August 2002 as a Chief Master Sergeant, the highest enlisted grade. He currently resides in San Antonio, Texas, where he's working on his first novel. He and his wife have been married thirty-two years and have three grown children and two grandchildren.

Laurie M. Doran ("Tying the Knot") is a freelance writer and photographer. She is a published author in *KnitLit* and *KnitLit (too)*. Laurie's feature articles and photographs have been published in many Maine newspapers and on the Internet. She lives in Maine with her husband, Roger.

Sandy Williams Driver ("Finicky Bride") and her husband, Tim, live in Albertville, Alabama, where both were born and raised. They have three children: Josh, Jake, and Katie. Sandy has been a full-time writer for three years. Her stories have been included in several magazines, newspapers, and anthologies.

Norma Favor ("Last on the List") attended one year at Bob Jones University, where she met her husband. They pastored together for twenty-five years. Norma loves relating family stories to her grandchildren.

Beth Gay ("The Little China Cup") is the editor of "The Family Tree," which can be found at *http://electric-scotland.com*. She also is a freelance writer, photographer, and editor.

Judyann Grant ("Off-Road Experience") is a freelance writer with twenty years of experience. She has been published in both fiction and nonfiction for children and adults, has three children's books under contract, and is working on a book of inspirational meditations for adults. She and her husband live in the small township of Mannsville, New York, and are the proud parents of three daughters and grandparents of three precious little granddaughters.

Nancy Gustafson ("When It Began") has published poetry and short fiction in anthologies and journals. She is retired from Sam Houston State University and lives with her husband, Jan, in Huntsville, Texas.

Maria Harden ("I Do") has been married for twenty-six years and has one son and one grandchild. She lives and works in Winnipeg, Manitoba. Maria and her husband love to travel.

Ann Hite ("Happily Ever After") has published numerous short stories and essays with publications like *The SiNk*, *Skyline Magazine*, *Wild Violet*, *Long Story Short*, *The Dead Mule*, *Foilate Oak*, and *Fiction Warehouse*. She is also a story editor with *Skyline Magazine*.

Wanda Huffstutter ("A Time to Treasure") was born in Fort Smith, Arkansas. She was married to a Navy man for forty years and was a seascape artist. Though she was married to her second husband, Bruce, for only seventeen months, she treasures the time they had together. Wanda has had articles published in various magazines, including *Country America*, *Angels on Earth*, and *The Ozark's Mountaineer*.

Linda Lipscomb Juergensen ("You Never Know") currently lives in Athol, Idaho, with her husband and three dogs, two cats, two horses, and seven alpacas. She recently retired from teaching junior high school and has taken up a career as a freelance writer. She holds a Master's in Education and a certificate in Technical Writing and belongs to the Idaho Writer's League of Coeur d'Alene, Idaho.

Emmarie Lehnick ("Will You?"), of Amarillo, Texas, is a retired English and speech teacher who holds both a bachelor's and master's degree. She and her husband have a daughter, a son, and four grandsons. She is a member of Inspirational Writers Alive and has stories published in several of the *Cup of Comfort* books and in other publications.

Hope Irvin Marston ("Unwilling Accomplice") is a retired teacher, librarian, and freelance writer, primarily of children's books. When she is not working at her computer, she can be found reading, making author appearances, doing research, or attending writing workshops as a presenter or a learner.

Karen Ott Mayer ("Worth the Risk") is an award-winning short fiction author and freelance publications writer based in north Mississippi. Her published works include essays, nonfiction articles, and short stories.

Walter McElligott ("Memories in the Making") is a freelance writer living in south suburban Chicago who has previously ghostwritten a supplement and a book on small-business tax law for a lawyer. He has written numerous articles, most recently a story on his wife Joan's healing from breast cancer. He and Joan, a retired special education teacher, have two children and five grandchildren.

Pat Capps Mehaffey ("Blind Date" and "An Ancient Treasure") is an ex-banker, retired to a lake home, where she enjoys birds, grandchildren, and writing. From the serenity of this location, Pat wrote and published two Christian editation books, has had stories published in several anthologies, and in 2003, won first place in a regional obituary-writing contest.

Lad Moore ("One Day in the Gulf of Georgia") enjoys hundreds of writing credits in print and on the Web, and has earned several awards, including a nomination to the Texas Institute of Letters. His work has appeared in such publications as *Virginia Adversaria, The Pittsburgh Quarterly, Paumanok Review, Carolina Country,* and *Amarillo Bay.* Lad is a four-time contributor to Adams Media anthologies, and is featured in an edition of *Chicken Soup for the Soul.* Two collections of his short stories, *Odie Dodie* and *Tailwind,* have been published by BeWrite-Jacobsen Books. Lad resides in Jefferson, Texas.

Bridget Balthrop Morton ("Blessed Be the Hem That Binds") published her first book, *Atlantic Cruising Club's Guide to East Coast Florida Marinas,* in March 2005. Her essays and poems have appeared in anthologies and magazines. She and her husband of thirty-five years live in Melbourne, Florida, where she writes and plays with her children and (so far) three grandchildren.

Rhoda Novak ("Momma Throws a Wedding") and John, her husband and college lab partner, are innovators in the aerospace industry in southern California. In addition to engineering and mentoring other engineers, Rhoda studies creative writing and quilt-making. Her award-winning work is published in magazines, poetry journals, anthologies, newspapers, engineering journals, and Web lit magazines. She enjoys weekly visits with her daughter, Jennifer, and grandchildren, Matthew and Sarah, time with John, and frequent phone calls to Momma.

Joseph K. Novara ("Let It Rest") lives in Kalamazoo, Michigan, and works in corporate communications when he is not writing for magazines or producing young adult novels and a collection of humorous horse stories.

Carol O'Dell ("The Flash of a Smile") has published work in numerous anthologies and magazines. Carol teaches creative writing at community centers, schools, and libraries. She is also an inspirational speaker on writing, caregiving, and adoption issues. Her Web site is *www.caroldodell.com*.

Sharon Cupp Pennington ("Dancing with My Best Friend") resides in Texas and is presently working on her first romantic suspense novel, *Hoodoo Money*. Her short stories have been published in *The Emporium Gazette*, *The Written Wisdom*, *Seasons for Writing*, *FlashQuake*, *Mocha Memoirs*, and *Flash Shots*.

Linda Kaullen Perkins ("Running Late") has published articles in newspapers, magazines, and anthologies, including *The Standard*, *Living*, *Country Woman*, and *Party Line*. She retired in 2001—after thirty-one years as an elementary teacher—and has since completed a young adult prairie adventure set in 1856 Missouri.

Rhonda Lane Phillips ("Not an Ordinary Patch of Grass") loves to revisit the mountain in West Virginia that she calls home. There, she remembers scenes from her youth and hears tales of years gone by, much of which becomes fodder for the stories she loves to write. In addition to being a writer, Rhonda is a reading specialist for a middle and high school, and mother of two teens.

Patsy Evans Pittman ("Seasons of Love") lives with her second husband, Stanley, in Vienna, West Virginia. Between them, they have four sons, two daughters, and fourteen grandchildren. Her stories, poems, and essays have appeared in a variety of regional and national periodicals, including *Ideals*, *Country Woman*, *First for Women*, and *Woman's World*, among others. Her short stories and essays have also been published in the following anthologies: *Guideposts for the Spirit—Stories for Sisters, Best of West Virginia Writers,* and *Confluence.*

Connie Vigil Platt ("I Married My High School Sweetheart") has been published in various anthology books, and in magazines such as *FATE Magazine* and *Woman's Day,* as well as *Dorchester Media.* She has also contributed to community cookbooks. Her novel *Pair a Dice* can be found at all major bookstores.

Kathryn Thompson Presley ("The Friendship Quilt"), a retired English professor, has published numerous short stories and poems. She loves reading, speaking to women's groups, and playing board games with her grandchildren. She has been married fifty-two years to Roy Presley, a retired school administrator.

Sheryl Puchalski ("Someone Old, Someone New") is a former elementary teacher originally from Hamburg, New York. She is now a proud stay-at-home mom of three young children, and resides in Tonawanda, New York. She and her husband, Tom, love camping and spend lots of time enjoying the outdoors with their children.

Dorothy Read ("Curfews and Credit Cards") is active in the nationally known Whidbey Island Writers' Association. Dorothy and her husband, Dean, live on Whidbey Island, in a woodsy retreat that is perfect for writing reminiscence.

Carol McAdoo Rehme (" . . . And Still Holding") is a freelance writer and editor. She publishes prolifically in the inspirational market. She also coauthored three books in 2003: *Angels Watching Over Us, Angels Book,* and *Journal, Blessings Book and Journal.*

Roberta Rhodes ("A Cut Above") was born on a farm in Iowa, grew up in Wyoming, and now lives and writes in Pennsylvania. She writes a regular column for *Tri-State*

Senior News and has been published in devotional publications as well as *Birds & Blooms* and *Mature Living*. She is a contributing writer to the *Erie* (Pennsylvania) *Times-News*.

Lee Rhuday ("Family Traditions," "Daddy's Little Girl"), writing under a pseudonym, is a member of Romance Writers of America and the Space Coast Writers' Guild. She lives in Central Florida, where she penned a monthly column for *The Sweat Gazette* until Florida's latest hurricane season put the newspaper out of business. Lee's primary interest is women's fiction. Currently she is working on a novel.

Cariad Rhys-Cook ("A God Thing"), writing under a pseudonym, finds real people and places the most rewarding. Her love of small towns and the lifestyles they offer, not to mention the characters often met in these unique places, are grist for the mill, and what has kept her writing since childhood.

Linda Rondeau ("A Blonde and a Boy Scout") has published nearly 100 manuscripts in traditional and online publications and features an inspirational humor column on her Web site, *www.lindarondeau.com*, called According to Daisy/Tips for Abundant Living. In addition, Linda writes a monthly humor column for the American Christian Fiction Writers newsletter, "According to Daisy/The Writer's Abundant Life."

Bob Rose ("Under the Cottonwood Tree") and his wife, Kathy, have three sons, two daughters-in-law, and six grandchildren. His publication credits include magazines such as *Home Life*, *Experiencing God*, *The Christian Communicator*, *Ideals*, and *Church Libraries*. He writes a weekly newspaper column, "Crossed Paths," which has appeared in numerous Texas newspapers and currently runs in the Rawlins, Wyoming *Daily Times*.

Nan Schindler Russell ("Falling in Love") is living her dream in Whitefish, Montana, after twenty years in management on the East Coast. Currently writing her first book, *Winning at Working: 10 Lessons Shared*, Nan is a writer, columnist, small business owner, and instructor. More of Nan's work can be read at *www.nanrussell.com*.

Dorothy Scearcy ("The Yellow Swimsuit") lives in Grove, Oklahoma, where she writes nostalgic stories for *The Webb City Sentinel* and *The Grand Lake Chronicle*. Dorothy began her writing career late in life but loves every moment of it.

Kimberly Shoemaker ("In Sickness and in Health") is published (under a pseudonym) in romance fiction with bestseller status for December 2004. She has served in various clinical and clerical positions in medical offices, including office supervisor.

Susan J. Siersma ("Love at First Suede Coat") is a native of New Jersey. Several of Susan's stories have been published in various anthologies. The inspiration for her work comes from everyday life and from the people around her. Besides writing, Susan enjoys organic gardening, time spent with her children and grandchildren, playing the violin, and long walks with her husband, Rodger.

Verna L. Simms ("Lucky in Love") is a retired librarian, a freelance writer, and a member of the Jefferson County Writers' Society. Verna and her husband were married on the outskirts of Festus, Missouri, in 1940. She has been happily married to the same man for sixty-four years. Together they have two daughters, four grandchildren, three great-grandchildren, and one great-great-grandchild.

Lou W. Souders ("My War Bride") and her husband John have three children and three grandchildren. Lou has been in ministry since 1980. Currently, she is speaking to Ladies Ministries on various topics including "Tea with the Master Potter" and "Stand by Your Man."

Lou is the owner of Teacup Traditions, a gift line centered on the cards and stories she writes. She can be found at *www.teacuptraditions.com*.

Judith Ann Squier ("The Best of All") resides in northern California with her husband, David, and their three grown daughters. Judith has been a public speaker since age thirteen and more recently a published writer.

Michele Starkey ("Saving Pennies") is a brain aneurysm survivor who enjoys writing and sharing her stories. She is living life to the fullest with her husband, Keith, in the Hudson Valley of New York State.

Mary Helen Straker ("The Getaway") formerly a newspaper and magazine reporter, has had her work published in both short fiction and nonfiction, and has had two short stories published in the *Cup of Comfort* series. She currently is working on a family memoir and has led a workshop in memoir writing at a Columbus, Ohio, library.

Barb Webb ("A Worthy Catch") currently resides in the South, but often returns to her beloved Land of 10,000 Lakes with a fishing pole in hand. For more of Barb's fish tales and additional information regarding her books, please visit her Web site at *www.barbwebb.com*.

Shirley H. Wetzel ("Two-Dollar Wife") is a librarian at Rice University. She was born in the small town of Comanche, Texas, and although she has lived in cities most of her life, her heart remains in the country. Shirley has strong interests in writing, genealogy, and family history and has begun compiling her family stories.

Garnet Hunt White ("A Magic Wedding Dress") is a retired schoolteacher. She lives outside the Doniphan, Missouri city limits. Garnet loves animals and takes care of stray dogs and cats. Her work has been published in a variety of publications.

Stella Ward Whitlock ("This Diamond Ring") is the wife of a retired Presbyterian minister, mother of four adult children, and grandmother to seven—five boys and two girls. Stella retired in 2000 after teaching public school for thirty-nine years. Currently she teaches writing at Methodist College, Fayetteville, North Carolina, and is fulfilling her dream of writing some of the many stories that have been passed down in her family.

Barbara K. Williams ("Huckleberry Romance") is a freelance writer from Fort Wayne, Indiana. She loves writing short stories about growing up in rural Indiana. Barb also writes church drama, skits, and retreat material for women's ministries. She has always been active in theater—from director to costumer—and enjoys art, reading, flowers, and her grandkids.

Linda M. Wolk ("A Dream Wedding") is an educator, having worked most of her thirty-seven years in the inner city of Boston with children with special needs. Currently Linda works part time for the Wellesley College "Open Circle" teacher education program, consulting with teachers and implementing a social skills and problem-solving curriculum with elementary-age students.

Carole Wyatt ("On Rodents Feet") is a high school special education teacher who resides in the small rural town of Clay City with her minister husband, three children, two dogs, one guinea pig, and assorted fish. In her leisure time, she gardens, writes, and reads almost everything she can get her hands on.

Leslie J. Wyatt ("Could Love Get Any Sweeter?") is a freelance writer. Her work has been accepted for publication in several anthologies, including *A Cup of Comfort for Courage*, and *My Heart's First Step*. In addition to numerous published articles and stories and business writing, her middle-grade historical novel is available from Holiday House, Inc.

Sharon Kingan Young ("Small Packages of Love") has lived in Iowa for twenty-nine years with her husband, Don. Together they have two children and three grandchildren. She has been published in magazines such as *The Iowan*, *ByLine*, *Collectors News*, *Wisconsin Trails*, and *GRIT*.

Kristine Ziemnik ("The Letter") lives with her husband, Joseph, in lovely, historic Chippewa Lake, Ohio. She owns a home-based craft business called Kristine's Kreations. Writing stories is another of her creative outlets.

Tell Your Story in the Next *Cup of Comfort*!

We hope you have enjoyed *A Cup of Comfort for Weddings* and that you will share it with all the special people in your life.

You won't want to miss our next heartwarming volumes, *A Cup of Comfort for Parents of Children with Autism* and *A Cup of Comfort Devotional for Mothers*. Look for these new books in your favorite bookstores soon!

We're brewing up lots of other *Cup of Comfort* books, each filled to the brim with true stories that will touch your heart and soothe your soul. The inspiring tales included in these collections are written by everyday men and women, and we would love to include one of your stories in an upcoming edition of *A Cup of Comfort*.

Do you have a powerful story about an experience that dramatically changed or enhanced your life? A compelling story that can stir our emotions, make us think, and bring us hope? An inspiring story that reveals lessons of humility within a vividly told tale? Tell us your story!

Each *Cup of Comfort* contributor will receive a monetary fee, author credit, and a complimentary copy of the book. Just e-mail your submission of 1,000 to 2,000 words (one story per e-mail; no attachments, please) to:

cupofcomfort@adamsmedia.com

Or, if e-mail is unavailable to you, send it to:

A Cup of Comfort
Adams Media
57 Littlefield Street
Avon, MA 02322

You can submit as many stories as you'd like, for whichever volumes you'd like. Make sure to include your name, address, and other contact information and indicate for which volume you'd like your story to be considered. We also welcome your suggestions or stories for new *Cup of Comfort* themes.

For more information, please visit our Web site: *www.cupofcomfort.com*.

We look forward to sharing many more soothing *Cups of Comfort* with you!

About the Editor

Helen Kay Polaski has always believed in magic, especially the kind that keeps marriages together, binds siblings and friends, and ties the concept of home close to the heart. Because she is the seventh child in a family of sixteen children and has more nieces and nephews than she can count, she has attended lots of weddings.

Helen hails from Metz, Michigan, a small town just sixty miles southeast of the Mackinac Bridge, where she met and married her high school sweetheart, Thomas. They have been married for thirty years and have three children: April, Alissa, and Nathan.

A retired journalist, Helen has compiled and edited six anthologies and written several screenplays.

The *Cup of Comfort* Series!

All titles are $9.95 unless otherwise noted.

A Cup of Comfort
1-58062-524-X

A Cup of Comfort Cookbook ($12.95)
1-58062-788-9

A Cup of Comfort Devotional ($12.95)
1-59337-090-3

A Cup of Comfort Devotional for Women ($12.95)
1-59337-409-7

A Cup of Comfort for Christians
1-59337-541-7

A Cup of Comfort for Christmas
1-58062-921-0

A Cup of Comfort for Friends
1-58062-622-X

A Cup of Comfort for Grandparents
1-59337-523-9

A Cup of Comfort for Inspiration
1-58062-914-8

A Cup of Comfort for Mothers and Daughters
1-58062-844-3

A Cup of Comfort for Mothers and Sons
1-59337-257-4

A Cup of Comfort for Mothers to Be
1-59337-574-3

A Cup of Comfort for Nurses
1-59337-542-5

A Cup of Comfort for Sisters
1-59337-097-0

A Cup of Comfort for Teachers
1-59337-008-3

A Cup of Comfort for Weddings
1-59337-519-0

A Cup of Comfort for Women
1-58062-748-X

A Cup of Comfort for Women in Love
1-59337-362-7